Ripples from Warwickshire's Past

PAUL BOLITHO

To my wife, Doreen, for all her help and encouragement

First published in 1992 by Warwickshire Books,
Department of Libraries and Heritage,
Barrack Street,
Warwick
CV34 4TH.
Tel (0926) 412659

Typeset in Baskerville by Carnegie Publishing Ltd, 18 Maynard St.,
Preston
Printed and bound in the UK by the Alden Press, Oxford

British Library Cataloguing-in-Publication Data
Bolitho, Paul
  Ripples from Warwickshire's Past
    1. Social Life, history
    I. Title
    920.04248

Contents

Foreword

PROMINENT figures of yesterday, as well as those of past centuries, may suffer utter, or partial, oblivion. Once, giving a talk on historic inn-signs, I mentioned the Jet and Whittle in Leamington Spa, only to be confronted with the query: 'What is a whittle?'. The questioner, not young, was perfectly serious; he had never heard of Coventry-born Sir Frank Whittle, inventor of the jet engine, and still with us! If there were a Scamp Arms anywhere, many folk would not be aware that the late Sir Jack Scamp, of Ufton, was an industrial troubleshooter of infinite skill, who would be more than welcome in a far wider sphere today!

Paul Bolitho, in these invaluable *Ripples from Warwickshire's Past*, has cast his net widely and well, reminding us of the brave, accomplished, notorious, or eccentric, always linked with our county. We read of Edward II's favourite, Piers Gaveston, and his grisly fate on Blacklow Hill, near Warwick, the monument there bearing an inscription (not entirely accurate) by the quaint, beloved Dr. Samuel Parr of Hatton. The splendid actress, Sarah Siddons, has perhaps little-known associations with now-ruined Guy's Cliffe, quite near that memorial; more readers may know of Leamington's intimate connections with lawn tennis - or perhaps not. Marie Corelli's once avidly-devoured novels are virtually forgotten, if her colourful career in Stratford-upon-Avon - Venetian gondola and all - stirs vague memories for some. We encounter enigmatic Frances, Countess of Warwick, on the hustings, like her friend, Joseph Arch, the agricultural labourers' champion who, alas, took to the whisky bottle; and 'Her Ladyship' (not 'Comrade Warwick', thank you, despite her politics) would undoubtedly have approved of Pat Arrowsmith, anti-nuclear campaigner. Poets - one ill-tempered - cartoonist, musician, heroic Czechs, Polar explorers, Warwickshire's first V.C., even the founder of a famous Cairo hotel, are all here. We may be surprised, momentarily horrified, occasionally amused, as we contemplate the many 'ripples' of Warwickshire's past.

Charles Lines, M.B.E.
Author of The Book of Warwick

Preface

ASKED to name famous men and women associated with Warwickshire, most people would suggest Shakespeare and possibly
George Eliot and Lady Godiva. But there have been many other
folk connected with the county who have left their mark upon the national scene. In this personal and by no means exhaustive selection of
portraits from the fourteenth century to the present day, the author
seeks to describe some of the less well-known yet significant characters
from the south of the county.

If Shakespeare's influence can be likened to a huge tidal wave, then
these people represent currents on the local pond, rippling outwards to
lap the very shores of our national life, and illustrate the diversity of
Warwickshire's contribution to British history.

Warwickshire (the old geographical county), showing places mentioned in the book.

— 1 —

Royal Favourite

F OR a short while, in the year 1312, Warwick was at the centre of our national political history: on a small hill just to the north of the town a certain notorious Piers Gaveston met an untimely end.

Edward II (who reigned from 1307 to 1327) was one of England's weakest kings, and his reliance on favourites ultimately led to his downfall and hideous murder. His first and greatest favourite was Piers Gaveston with whom he became particularly intimate.

Piers was the son of a Gascon knight from the south west of France whom Edward I appointed as one of the royal wards - the official companions of his son. So, unwittingly, Dad really began it all; indeed, just before he died he must have begun to have his doubts about their friendship because he saw fit to banish Gaveston from the country. Piers was not quite such an upstart as the jealous barons liked to claim. As for being a foreigner, as they alleged, many families in the post-Norman Middle Ages had French connections. Moreover, he does indeed seem to have been a personable and charming young man. On his accession in 1307, Edward II immediately recalled Gaveston, created him Earl of Cornwall (a title customarily reserved for a member of the royal family) and married him to his niece. This is when Gaveston's arrogance became apparent and alienated the barons, especially when he gave them nicknames injurious to their pride and deflating to their dignity. In particular, Guy Beauchamp, Earl of Warwick, became 'the Black Dog of Arden' because of his swarthy complexion. The Earl vowed that one day Gaveston would feel the dog's teeth! For the time being the barons forced the king to banish him again to govern Ireland ('that vile torpedo Gaveston, that now I hope floats on the Irish seas' - Marlowe.) Needless to say, he was soon back.

Things came to a head in 1311 when the barons insisted on forty-one Ordinances to reform the government, the twentieth of which stated that Gaveston had 'misled and ill-advised our lord the King, and enticed him to do evil in various deceitful ways', and decreed that 'as an open enemy of the King and his people Gaveston shall be altogether exiled from England, Scotland, Ireland and Wales, and from all the dominion of our lord the King, both on this side and the other side of the sea'. No more comfortable sojourn in Ireland in royal state!

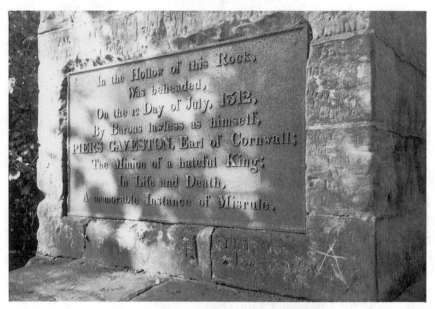

The Gaveston monument on Blacklow Hill.

Restless on the continent, however, Gaveston soon returned from this third exile and rejoined the King. This time both sides prepared for war, the barons gathering superior forces. King and favourite, in the north of England, escaped from Newcastle just in time to avoid capture. Gaveston took refuge in his own castle of Scarborough while Edward retired to York. But within a fortnight supplies at Scarborough ran out, and on 19 May 1312 Gaveston was obliged to surrender to the moderate Earl of Pembroke who assured him of his personal safety. According to the more charitable view Pembroke was a man of honour who expected to find similar honour in his brother earls. He took it upon himself to escort the royal favourite to his own castle of Wallingford where he would remain in custody until Parliament assembled. By the evening of 9 June the leisurely cavalcade had reached Deddington, half-a-dozen miles south of Banbury, where Pembroke lodged his prisoner in a lightly-guarded rectory while he went to spend the night with his wife at his manor of Bampton a few miles away. Little did he suspect that one of his more implacable colleagues might take the law into his own hands. But that is exactly what the Earl of Warwick did. Early in the morning of 10 June 'the Black Dog of Arden' and his men surrounded Deddington rectory and entered the house to wake Gaveston with the words, 'Get up, traitor, you are taken!'

Hustled out of the house, Gaveston was forced to walk barefoot for several miles towards Warwick. Eventually, more to speed things up than out of compassion, his captors put him on horseback, and as soon as they reached Warwick Castle he was thrown into a dungeon.

On returning to Deddington and finding his prisoner gone Pembroke is said to have been very angry – not that he had any tender feelings towards him, but because he had taken an oath to protect him. He tried to get help to persuade Warwick to release Gaveston, but to no avail: he had to stand helplessly by while events took their course.

Honourable and disillusioned Pembroke? However, another plausible view, both then and since, was that Pembroke's actions were not above suspicion. After all, was it merely an accident that he had left Gaveston so comparatively near Warwick with such an inadequate guard? Might it not have been on purpose? One likes to think not. But the truth was that all the earls secretly wished for Gaveston's death and yet none of them wanted to be implicated!

With Gaveston now in his clutches, Warwick was joined in the castle by his fellow Earls of Lancaster, Hereford and Arundel. According to one account they went to the trouble of finding two justices to pronounce sentence. Since he was Earl of Cornwall, whether they liked it or not, they agreed that he should die as a nobleman – by beheading instead of hanging. Accordingly, on 19 June he was brought up out of the dungeon and marched to Blacklow Hill, outside the town, a spot within the jurisdiction of the Earl of Lancaster, whose royal blood they thought would shield him from the king's anger. There, while Warwick remained in the castle, and Lancaster, Hereford and Arundel watched from a distance, Gaveston was beheaded as a traitor before a large crowd.

Accounts of the disposal of the body are macabre. The executioners left it where it had fallen. Four cobblers took up the headless corpse and carried it into town on a ladder to the Earl of Warwick. He, however, refused to receive it as he did not wish to bear any responsibility for what had happened and ordered them to return it to Blacklow Hill, so that it remained outside his territory. The shoemakers, with strange solicitude, then sewed the head back upon the body when they returned it. Ultimately a group of Dominicans (there was a house of the Black Friars outside the west gate of the town, from which Friars Street gets its name) took the body to their house in Oxford, one chronicler confusingly reporting that the head was carried by a friar in the hood of his cloak. At Oxford the corpse was dressed in cloth of gold and embalmed with balsam and spices, but it remained unburied since Gaveston had died under Archbishop Winchelsey's excommunication. Later, when the excommunication had been lifted, the King gave his friend a magnificent funeral early in January 1315 in the church of the Dominican priory of King's Langley in Hertfordshire.

The other actors in this drama ultimately fared no better than Gaveston himself. The King, as is well known, was foully murdered in Berkeley Castle in 1327. The Earl of Lancaster's royal blood did not save him from execution either; Pembroke was stabbed to death by a paid assassin; Hereford was killed in battle; and Arundel was beheaded. As for Guy Beauchamp, Earl of Warwick, he was poisoned in revenge by one of Gaveston's adherents. An inn at Southam a few miles from Leamington bears the name of The Black Dog, commemorating the execution on Blacklow Hill.

Inn sign of The Black Dog at Southam.

A monument surmounted by a cross, now little cared for, was erected on the site of Gaveston's execution in 1821 by Bertie Greatheed of Guy's Cliffe, the nearby mansion. It bears the inscription, composed by Dr Samuel Parr, Rector of Hatton: 'In the hollow of this rock was beheaded on the 1st day of July 1312, by barons lawless as himself, Piers Gaveston, Earl of Cornwall, the minion of a hateful king. In life and death, a memorable instance of misrule.' Unfortunately Samuel Parr got the date wrong. Gaveston was executed on what was then 19 June. It was decided to convert the date from the Old Style to the New Style - Britain had changed within living memory in 1752, from the Julian to the Gregorian calendar - when the days between 2 and 14 September had been omitted - so the erectors of the monument added twelve days to get to 1 July. But they forgot that the difference between the two styles would only have been eight days way back in 1312: they should have put 27 June. It would have been better to have kept to the Old Style for the older dates, as we do now.

If the monument is neglected, so is the way up. Take the Leek Wootton road at the roundabout and immediately turn left, doubling back and parking at the end of the cul-de-sac (if you are walking, there is a path from the road up to the cul-de-sac). Take the overgrown path on the side of the hill, cross the fence and go through the trees until you come across the monument on the edge of the copse looking towards Warwick. Wear boots - it can be muddy! But if you go in early spring you'll be rewarded with a superb carpet of snowdrops!

— 2 —

Gunpowder, Treason and Plot

E VERYONE knows that the Gunpowder Plot was a terrorist attempt by extreme Catholics to throw the government of the country into confusion by blowing up King James I together with Lords and Commons at the State Opening of Parliament. It is not so well known that the peaceful Warwickshire countryside played an important part in the drama, and that many of the conspirators were either Warwickshire born or Warwickshire based. Their leader, Robert Catesby, formerly of Bushwood Hall, Lapworth, masterminded operations from his mother's home at Ashby St Ledgers, just over the Northamptonshire border. Other conspirators included John Grant of Northbrook, a small estate between Warwick and Stratford; Ambrose Rookwood who conveniently rented Clopton House, Stratford; John Wright who rented Bushwood Hall; and Sir Everard Digby of Coleshill who found it convenient to stay with Throckmorton relatives at Coughton Court - Thomas Throckmorton was abroad at the time, though he may well have known of the plot. But of all the group the single-minded, utterly ruthless Catesby was undoubtedly the driving force: he had been involved some four years before in the abortive coup by the Earl of Essex against the aged Queen Elizabeth; he had schemed for a Spanish invasion; and he had even sold his property of Chastleton House just over the border in Oxfordshire to raise funds for the Gunpowder Plot.

The idea seems to have been that, following the success of the plot, there would be a general uprising, and, with the King and his two sons dead, the nine-year-old Princess Elizabeth (later in life a staunch Protestant!) would be seized at Combe Abbey, near Coventry, and proclaimed queen. In this madcap scheme the zealots felt that the hands of moderate Catholics would be forced since the consequent Protestant backlash would compel them all to defend themselves by force of arms from being massacred. Horses and arms and ammunition were stock-piled at various houses on pretence that it was for volunteer service in the Netherlands, and sympathetic Catholic gentry of the Midlands were to

Guy Fawkes' House at Dunchurch, formerly The Lion Inn.

meet on Dunsmore Heath, near Rugby, under cover of a hunting party. Amid the secrecy some knew more than others, some were innocently drawn in.

But the MI5 of the day got to know: King James's chief minister, the Earl of Salisbury, had his spies well placed. The traditional story is that one of the conspirators, Francis Tresham, sent his friend Lord Mounteagle a cryptic letter suggesting that he absent himself from the opening of Parliament (despite the fact that he and the others had acquiesced in Catesby's insistence that no one should be warned: regretfully a few dead Catholics must be the price to secure the success of the enterprise). 'They shall receive a terrible blow this Parliament', wrote Tresham, 'and they shall not see who hurts them.' Mounteagle passed the letter on to the authorities. Alternatively, the letter could have been a government 'plant' to give the King the credit for 'discovering' the plot: counter-espionage probably knew of the existence of the plot long before, and the government bided its time until the very last moment and then pounced, in order to make the maximum amount of political capital and implicate the Jesuit priests too.

Initially only the loyal workhorse Guy Fawkes was arrested - in the cellars guarding the explosives during the night of 4–5 November. The rest of the conspirators on learning of his arrest behaved like fools.

With no chance of success they should have fled the country while the going was good: it was forty-eight hours before the proclamation was issued for the arrest of some but not all the conspirators, and it was five days before Fawkes confessed all under torture. Yet his colleagues did not take the opportunity of this slim chance to escape. Instead they proceeded with the second stage of their plan.

Catesby and his friends covered the eighty miles from London to Ashby in seven hours using relays of horses, and then joined the hundred huntsmen who had gathered for their pre-arranged supper on the evening of 5 November in the Lion Inn at Dunchurch. Disheartened, all but thirty or forty of them dispersed. Catesby proposed that this small band should make for Wales, trying to collect reinforcements on the way – a hopeless venture, as it turned out. They left Dunchurch at about 10 p.m. Proceeding by way of Bourton Heath, they crossed the Fosse Way at Princethorpe and continued by way of Wappenbury, Weston-under-Wetherley and Lillington. Arriving about midnight at Warwick – where only the year before the quarters of a Catholic priest had been displayed on the town gates – they broke into some stables (where exactly is unknown) and stole fresh horses, leaving their tired ones behind in exchange. They collected some more weapons from John Grant's house at Northbrook, leaving there at dawn next day and travelling westwards by way of Snitterfield and Alcester. Catesby's servant, Thomas Bates, was sent to break the news to the ladies waiting at Coughton Court: you can still see the room over the archway (the property now belongs to the National Trust) where they awaited the success but were told of the failure of their menfolk. Eventually, irresolute and demoralized and with self-inflicted injuries from trying to dry damp gunpowder, the conspirators were cornered by government forces on 8 November in Holbeach House, near Dudley, and after a brief fight Catesby and some of the others were killed. The rest were captured and, with others rounded up elsewhere, were later tried and executed.

The old Lion Inn in Dunchurch is no longer an inn, but it is still standing and goes by the name of Guy Fawkes House. Despite the fact that Guy Fawkes himself never went near the place, it is perhaps a fitting name by which to remember the famous rendezvous.

— 3 —

A King's Last Word

I N the very south of Warwickshire, in the village of Little Compton, the church of St Denis with its saddle-back tower contains a handsome stained-glass window in a south chapel depicting the last hours and burial of King Charles I.

A picture of Christ's crucifixion forms the centre light. On the left, the window bearing the date January 29, 1649 has a smaller upper light showing Charles I saying farewell to his children with a certain clergyman in attendance, and a larger lower light depicting Charles and the same clergyman walking through the snow. On the right, the window bears the date January 30, 1649 and has a smaller upper light showing the King on the scaffold talking to the clergyman with the executioner in the background, and a larger lower light depicting the clergyman escorting the King's coffin through the snow to St George's Chapel, Windsor, where he was forbidden to conduct the burial service from the *Prayer Book*.

Whatever the previous conduct of the King, there can be no doubt of his bravery as he stepped out of the Banqueting House window of Whitehall Palace on to the scaffold on that icy January day: secretly he wore two shirts so that he should not shiver and be accused of fear. He was encouraged by that clergyman beside him, his chaplain, William Juxon, Bishop of London, who at the King's request had voluntarily shared his captivity during his trial. Amid the roll of drums, Juxon said to his King, 'There is but one stage more, which though turbulent and troublesome, yet is a very short one; you may consider it will soon carry you a very great way; it will carry you from Earth to Heaven, and there you will find a crown of glory'. The King replied, 'I go from a corruptible to an incorruptible Crown'. Then followed his enigmatic last word: 'Remember!' We do not know what we were to remember, but we do know to whom it was spoken - the mild-mannered William Juxon, who afterwards retired to Little Compton, then in Gloucestershire but now in Warwickshire. Hence the church window, which was designed between the wars by artist Hugh Easton.

William Juxon was born in 1582. He became Vicar of St Giles's, Oxford, Rector of Somerton, President of St John's (succeeding his friend

*The church window at Little Compton which depicts the execution
and burial of Charles I.*

Laud in 1621) and Vice-Chancellor of Oxford University. He was also
Dean of Worcester for a short time, and he succeeded Laud as Bishop
of London in 1633. He also became Lord High Treasurer in 1636. Those
were the days when the Lord High Treasurer was as important an office as the Chancellor of the Exchequer is today. In Juxon's case it was
felt that as a clergyman and a bachelor he would be above the tempta-
tions which had led his predecessors to enrich themselves at the ex-
pense of the state.

Before becoming President of St John's, where he built an attractive
quadrangle, Juxon acquired the manor house at Little Compton, which

had once belonged to Tewkesbury Abbey, and remodelled it extensively. Deprived of his bishopric by a Presbyterian Parliament (he had resigned as Treasurer in 1641), it was to this quiet place that he retired during the Commonwealth. He spent a lot of his time hunting. One writer tells us that he had 'a pack of good hounds and had them so well ordered and hunted, chiefly by his own skill and direction, that they exceeded all hounds in England for the pleasure and orderly hunting of them'. The writer concerned added quaintly that 'he had as much command of himself as of his hounds'.

Juxon used to conduct the banned Church of England service in neighbouring Chastleton House, the mansion that Robert Catesby had sold fifty years earlier to provide funds for the Gunpowder Plot. Both Bible and execution block used on that fateful day in January are said to have been kept at Chastleton at one time.

At the Restoration in 1660 Juxon was made Archbishop of Canterbury at the age of seventy-eight and, though a sick man, crowned his master's son as King Charles II in Westminster Abbey. The pleasure-loving young monarch, it is said, 'treated him with outward respect, but had no great regard to him' and Juxon, 'after some discourses with the King, was so much struck with what he observed in him that he lost both heart and hope'. He died shortly afterwards, in 1663, but not before he had been responsible for rebuilding the fine hall of Lambeth Palace, the official residence of successive archbishops. Little Compton church has Juxon gravestones in the nave, but the archbishop himself is interred beside Laud in St John's College. The manor house was for a while the home of Major Edward 'Fruity' Metcalfe, best man and equerry to the Duke of Windsor – another indirect royal connection. Today it is a college of accountancy. With a panelled upstairs 'Juxon Room', it stands in formal gardens with an enclosure for a herd of deer said to be descended from some that were there in Juxon's time.

As for Juxon himself, he was a man of principle, but forbearing in an age of intolerance. To quote from the *Dictionary of National Biography*:

As a churchman Juxon was simple, spiritual and sincere. He held the views of Laud as to the constitution and order of the Church, but enforcing ecclesiastical ordinances with tact and discretion. As a statesman he was laborious rather than original, carrying out a system, with which there is no reason to think that he was not in full agreement, as far as possible without friction. Strong and loyal, self-contained yet sympathetic, he was one of the few men in times of strife of whom it may be said that they made no enemies. His best character was that which his royal master, King Charles I, gave him, 'that good man'.

— 4 —

Organist and Composer

A younger contemporary of Henry Purcell, William Croft is Warwickshire's most famous musician. He came from Ettington, near Stratford, and is known today mainly for his hymn tunes and the renowned music for the Burial Service.

Dr Croft had a distinguished pedigree. Both he and the Crofts of Croft Castle in Herefordshire were descended from Bernard de Croft who held the castle at the time of the Domesday Book, and from Sir John de Croft who married a daughter of Owen Glendower, the Welsh prince. His grandfather William married Margaret, daughter of the Greek scholar Francis Hyckes, who with his father Richard designed and executed some of the famous Sheldon tapestries at Barcheston in the south of the county.

Some time before 1670 William and Margaret's son, another William, came to the manor of Nether Eatington, the house of the ancient Shirley family. Ettington, as it is now spelt and has always been pronounced, consisted at that time of two hamlets, Over and Nether Eatington. Here in 1671 this William married Jane Brent, daughter of the former vicar, and on 30 December 1678 their son, a third William, was baptized.

Alas, in 1798 the hamlet of Nether Eatington (the area was later known as Lower Ettington, then as Ettington Park and the manor is now a country hotel) was demolished to make way for a deer park. The inhabitants moved to the larger village of Over Eatington, now simply known as Ettington. The manor house where the composer was born can no longer be seen because it was enclosed and roofed over in the mid nineteenth century in Victorian Gothic, though what was once a private chapel at the rear can still be seen. The nearby church where Croft was baptized is now a ruin: only the south transept is in good repair as the mortuary chapel of the Shirley family, who also left a small marble urn there as a memorial to the composer.

When he was four years old his family moved to Tredington, a few miles away, where his father became churchwarden. But it is thought that William's taste for music might have been nurtured by attendance at services at Holy Trinity, Stratford, where a cousin was vicar and where the quality of the music was probably higher.

William Croft's hymn tune 'Eatington'.

At about eight years of age he became a choirboy at the Chapel Royal where Henry Purcell was organist and John Blow was Master of the Children, i.e. the choirboys. The Chapel Royal was not a building but a body of clergy and musicians which met in the chapel of Whitehall Palace until most of that palace burned down in 1698, and then in the chapel of St James's Palace. Here the boys were not only taught to sing but also the three Rs, Latin, the organ and the harpsichord. Croft continued at the chapel even after his voice had broken, probably serving an apprenticeship with Blow as organist and composer until he left temporarily at the age of twenty. In 1700 he was appointed organist of St Anne's, Soho, and in the same year rejoined the Chapel Royal after a short break as Gentleman Extraordinary, i.e. choirman. Four years later he became joint organist there with Jeremiah Clarke (composer of the 'Trumpet Voluntary') and sole organist in 1707 on Clarke's suicide after an unhappy love affair. On the death of his mentor Blow in the following year Croft succeeded him as Master of the Children at the royal chapel, as composer to the Queen, and as organist at Westminster Abbey. So by the age of thirty he was the leading church musician of his day.

Dr Croft had married Mary George of Kensington in 1704. They had no family of their own, but in his capacity as Master of the Children he had ten choirboys to look after.

Croft's secular output dates from his twenties: sonatas, songs such as 'By Purling Streams', and theatrical accompaniments for various contemporary plays at Drury Lane. The youthful freshness of these pieces contrasts with the solemnity he was later to adopt, but it was as a composer of sacred music that he excelled.

His duties included the writing of official works to be performed in Westminster Abbey or St Paul's on historic occasions - thanksgivings for Marlborough's victories of Blenheim, Ramillies, Oudenarde and Malplaquet (his 'Festival Te Deum and Jubilate in D' was composed for the last named), the funeral of Queen Anne, the suppression of the Jacobite Rising of 1715, and the coronations of George I and George II, the last of which he did not live to see. Other large-scale works for soloists, chorus and orchestra were his 'Academic Odes' which were performed in Oxford's Sheldonian Theatre to celebrate the Peace of Utrecht in 1713 when Croft took his D.Mus. degree.

He also wrote over ninety anthems, thirty of the best appearing in a major two-volume work *Musica Sacra* in 1724, a publication which also included his music for the Burial Service which has been used ever since at state and other choral funerals. It was Croft's anthem 'Out of the deep have I called unto Thee, O Lord' which John Wesley heard in St Paul's Cathedral in the afternoon of that day in May 1738 when a few hours later his heart was 'strangely warmed' and Methodism was born.

But it is perhaps Croft's hymn tunes which are best known. Foremost among them, named after his Soho church, is 'St Anne' ('O God, our Help in ages past'). Then there is the appropriately named 'Eatington' ('Happy the Souls to Jesus joined') and 'Hanover' ('O Worship the King, all glorious above'), 'St Matthew' ('Thine Arm, O Lord, in days of old'), 'Binchester' ('Happy are they, They that love God') and 'Croft's 136th' ('Ye Holy Angels Bright').

In 1727, because of illness, he went to Bath to take the waters, but to no avail; he died there in his fiftieth year. He was buried in the north aisle of Westminster Abbey, close to Blow and Purcell. A monument was erected to his memory by Humphrey Wyrley Birch, a lawyer whose family also came from Warwickshire. The epitaph states that Croft's music was excellently recommended 'by the force of his ingenuity, the sweetness of his manners and even of his countenance,' and that he showed 'a friendship and love truly paternal towards all whom he had instructed'.

— 5 —

Gardener to Queen Anne

H ENRY WISE, royal gardener, came to live in Warwick on his retirement. He had been an exponent of the formal garden and *parterre* or ornamental flowerbed. Born in 1653, he lived most of his life at his Brompton Park nursery, near London. Shortly after her accession, Queen Anne, who for all her thrift and caution was quite prepared to spend considerable sums of money on royal gardens, appointed Wise to manage the parks and gardens at St James, Kensington, Hampton Court and Windsor. He was also chosen by the Marlboroughs to lay out the parks and gardens at Blenheim and to dig the foundations for the house there. Whether in royal or ducal employ, he found himself working with such colleagues as Sir John Vanbrugh, Nicholas Hawksmoor and Grinling Gibbons. He was also commissioned to work on gardens at Chatsworth, Longleat and Melbourne.

After the death of the Queen things did not go so well for Wise. George I placed Vanbrugh over him – additional layers of management, apparently, not being peculiar to the late twentieth century – and he finally retired to Warwick in 1727 on the death of his tenant at the Priory, a mansion he had bought nearly twenty years before as insurance for his old age. It was a mansion with a history: sited on a twelfth-century priory; rebuilt by a Tudor developer called Thomas Hawkins who had purchased it from the Crown after the Dissolution of the Monasteries; visited by Queen Elizabeth I on one of her royal progresses; and later owned by a speaker of the House of Commons.

Wise was now seventy-four and an invalid. He was content to leave the house unaltered, but he was not, however, too infirm to redesign the garden. David Green describes his plan which has fortunately survived:

It shows an irregular composition formalized insofar as the existing contours allowed. The house is on the crest of a hill, with barely enough plateau to permit a terraced *parterre a l'anglaise.* On the west, before the main entrance-court, a plain oval of grass divides the carriage-way. On the east a thick semi-circular plantation – 'a pleasant grove of loftie elms' – is reinforced to protect six large formal

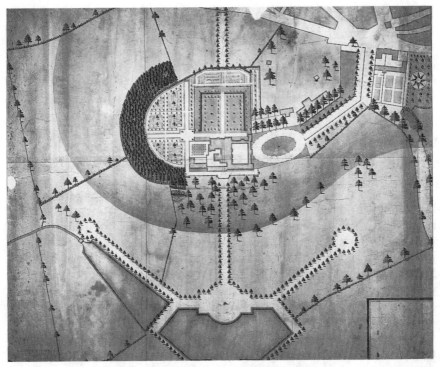

Henry Wise's plan of the Priory Garden, Warwick.

beds; while on the north a newly planted avenue, with curious formal offshoots, leads from the terrace down to distant and elaborate
waterworks in the form of two vast pools of geometrical design.

With the exception of these northern waterworks, the whole of
Wise's scheme, in the ten or eleven years of his retirement, would
appear to have been carried out. Considered from the plan, it is not
an exciting layout...Yet it would be unfair to judge without walking
in the garden as it was...The semi-circular garden on the east, hid-
den by its walls of elms and reminiscent of the Great Fountain Garden at Hampton Court, must have meant blissful seclusion to the old
gardener wheeled along its sanded paths...If he tired of that place
he might take to the southern terrace, with its magnificent view of
the tower of St Mary's and the Castle beyond.

If Wise had been younger or lived longer, he would surely have
struck out more boldly here. As it is, one examines his plan in vain
for any startling feature, old or new. It is the garden of an aged
formalist content with prospect, privacy and protection...There is
nothing to suggest that Wise in old age is taking to landscape gardening.

Two black stone slabs in the floor near the west door of St Mary's Church in Warwick bear the names of Henry Wise and his wife Patience, though their vault was at the entrance to the choir. His coat of arms bore a rose clutched in a lion's paw. Alas, soon after his death in 1738 men like Capability Brown with their new ideas on landscape gardening destroyed Wise's best work, and only Melbourne Hall in Derbyshire survives as an example of a French formal garden.

As for his legacy to Warwick itself, his garden was gradually obliterated. And the coming of the railway in 1851 cut through the Wise estate, severing the Priory from their Woodcote and Woodloes lands to the north, and Henry Christopher Wise, the royal gardener's great-great-grandson, sold the Priory in disgust, building himself a comfortable house at Woodcote instead. The Priory eventually passed into the hands of the Lloyds of the banking family, but by the beginning of this century its days were numbered. When the last owner moved out the place became derelict. It was bought by wealthy Americans, Mr and Mrs Alexander Weddell, in 1925, and then dismantled stone by stone, shipped across the Atlantic and re-erected in Richmond, Virginia, not as an exact replica of the Priory, but with recognizable features outside and the main staircase and stained glass inside. It is now the property of the Virginia Historical Society. At the time few people had a good word to say for the Weddells, but Warwickians did virtually nothing to save the mansion for the town, and apparently much of the material would have been used for the building of a factory if a local contractor had been the successful purchaser! *The Daily Mail* said that it was a scandal that the government allowed such things to happen, while *The Irish News* declared that 'among certain thoughtful people…the removal of the Priory is regarded as a really important indication of the degeneration and approaching downfall of Christian civilisation in the southern part of Great Britain'. But Pevsner said, 'good luck to them [the Weddells], considering the losses by neglect, vandalism and impoverishment that the major houses of England suffer every year'.

It is some consolation that the County Record Office (which houses Wise's plan) appropriately now stands on the site. And if little trace of Henry Wise's garden remains, at least the terracing has left pleasant steep banks in what is now a public park.

— 6 —

A Lady's Companion

THE Kembles were a famous theatrical family, including among their number Sarah (who later became Sarah Siddons), her brother John Philip Kemble and her niece Fanny Kemble. But Sarah was undoubtedly the greatest.

The young actress would have been well known to Warwick theatre-goers. Born in July 1755 in Brecon in mid Wales, she spent her childhood travelling in her father Roger Kemble's company of players, which was known as 'The Warwick Company of Comedians' at a time when theatrical performances were regarded as either tragedies or comedies. They performed in Coventry, Warwick and elsewhere, the theatre in Warwick being situated three doors along from the Globe Hotel – hence Theatre Street and particularly Theatre Court. Her father did not approve of Sarah's attachment to William Siddons, a member of the company. In an attempt to break up the romance, William was sacked, and Roger obtained a situation for Sarah at Guy's Cliffe, just outside Warwick, as lady's maid or companion to Lady Mary Greatheed, the widow of Samuel Greatheed who had built the house. It is said that Sarah used to recite Milton and Shakespeare in the servants' hall. However, her father's stratagem was unsuccessful: William and the eighteen-year-old Sarah were married by licence in Holy Trinity Church, Coventry, in November 1773, William having fetched his bride from Guy's Cliffe in a chaise. Father apparently acquiesced, because he signed the marriage register as a witness. The actors were then appearing at the Drapers' Hall in the city in dramatist-architect Vanbrugh's *The Provoked Husband* and the entire cast attended the wedding. William and Sarah had five children, but perhaps Sarah should have paid more heed to her father's objections, because the marriage was not very happy and eventually the couple lived apart, although they were never divorced.

Sarah went on to become a great actress at Drury Lane, famed for such parts as Lady Macbeth and immortalized as Sir Joshua Reynolds' 'Tragic Muse'. Hazlitt said of her: 'Power was seated on her brow; passion emanated from her breast as from a shrine. She was tragedy personified ... To have seen Mrs. Siddons was an event in everyone's life'.

Guy's Cliffe in its heyday.

In her great days she became an honoured guest at Guy's Cliffe, and today the public house on the neighbouring Woodloes Park estate bears her name.

Bertie Greatheed, Mary's son, who was responsible for erecting the Gaveston monument, had aspirations to be a playwright and wrote a drama called *The Regent.* Unfortunately it had the shortest of runs at Drury Lane. The principal roles were taken by John Kemble and Sarah Siddons, a trouper determined to tread the boards even though she was expecting a baby. 'After the second night,' wrote Greatheed in his journal, 'Mrs. Siddons miscarried ... and the play was arrested for that season. I had named it "Don Manuel". Mrs. Siddons thought "The Regent" a better title: we have had a regency almost ever since, and as my Regent is a villain, the play cannot be acted.' He added that Sarah took the play to Windsor to read it to the royal family 'when one of the King's first paroxysms came on and she was prevented'. And with the advent of George III's madness, it would have been scarcely tactful to offend the Prince Regent!

Today the Guy's Cliffe that Sarah knew is a ruin. Vacated by the Greatheeds' successors, the Percys, about 1939, it served as a boys' school during the Second World War. Subsequently stripped by speculative builders, the estate is now owned by the Freemasons who lovingly restored the chapel and adjacent rooms. The chapel is unique in serving both as a masonic temple and a consecrated building where marriages have taken place.

Unfortunately, the ruined house was accidentally damaged still further in 1992. Granada TV staff were using gas flames to simulate a blaze during the night-shooting of a Sherlock Holmes film, when the special effects went disastrously wrong. The house was engulfed in flames which took firefighters ten hours to control!

— 7 —

The Whig Dr Johnson

DR Samuel Parr (1747-1825) was a high-flier who, to use the modern jargon, decided to opt out of the rat-race at an early age, and for the last forty years of his life was content to be the vicar (or 'perpetual curate') of Hatton, near Warwick. Some of his contemporaries regarded him as the greatest scholar of his age, and he has been labelled by posterity 'the Whig Dr Johnson' because he was as prominent a scholar on the Radical side as Samuel Johnson was on the Tory. He was an eccentric character who was an ardent champion of civil and religious liberty. He was also notorious as a left-wing parson - which probably explains why he never got to the top of the ladder to become a bishop.

Parr did not in fact know Samuel Johnson very well, but in one argument with him on the freedom of the press 'I gave no quarter,' said Dr Parr, 'for Dr Johnson was very great. Whilst he was arguing I observed he stamped. Upon this, I stamped too. Dr Johnson said, "Why did you stamp, Dr Parr?" I replied, "Because you stamped, and I was resolved not give you the advantage even of a stamp in the argument."'

Parr was educated at Harrow and Emmanuel College, Cambridge, and became an assistant master at the school. In 1771 at the age of twenty-four he was an unsuccessful candidate for the post of headmaster there. Probably his youth told against him, possibly also the fact that he had voted for the Radical John Wilkes in the famous Middlesex election. Parr resigned as assistant master on being told that he was not being appointed headmaster, but with the satisfaction of knowing that the senior boys had petitioned the governors to reconsider their decision, so popular was he.

However, from 1771 to 1785 Parr held three other headships. First of all he set up his own school in an empty house in Stanmore, taking forty Harrow pupils with him. There followed headmasterships of Colchester and Norwich Grammar Schools. In 1783 he was appointed to the perpetual curacy of Hatton, and he took up residence there early in 1786 after resigning his Norwich appointment. He took on a variety of private pupils - some spared the horrors of the public schools, some who had already sampled them or had been expelled, and some past their schooldays who just wanted some final cramming of Latin and

Greek to enter university. Even so, Parr was to keep up his outside contacts for the rest of his life and he often revisited Cambridge and London.

At Hatton Parr was a model pastor of his flock, devoted to his parishioners. (His rectory is now a private dwelling and his church was largely rebuilt in 1880.) As a scholar he had a library of 10000 volumes. He composed the Latin inscription to Dr Johnson in St Paul's Cathedral, and, locally, the inscription on the Gaveston monument. He was a frequent visitor to the Greatheeds of Guy's Cliffe. He was in favour of religious toleration and among his friends were the Nonconformist divine William Field, who became his biographer, and John and William Parkes, pillars of Field's church in Warwick and owners of a worsted factory there. In 1824 John Parkes' son Joseph was married by Samuel Parr to Elizabeth, the grand-daughter of Dr Joseph Priestley; they were to become the maternal grandparents of Hilaire Belloc.

Samuel Parr was also a regular visitor to Warwick prison. He advocated reform of the criminal law: he wanted the death penalty reserved for treason and murder only. Above all he was an ardent Whig - Charles James fox was his political hero. He expressed progressive if cautious views on parliamentary reform. He was in favour of 'some well-directed and well-proportioned alteration in the influence of the Crown, in the authority of Parliament, and in the representation of the people', but yet recoiled from equal suffrage, 'one man, one vote'. Nevertheless he held that the most extreme of democrats had a right to be heard.

Twice the possibility of preferment might have occurred, but passed him by. In 1788-9 the King went mad, and it was anticipated that the Prince of Wales, at odds with his father, might favour those in opposition. But the King soon recovered. The second occasion was when the coalition Ministry of All the Talents was formed in 1806, but by then Fox was a dying man. So Parr was destined to remain a lowly curate.

His biographer writes that Samuel Parr used to be seen 'on the road from Hatton to Warwick, the most grotesque figure imaginable, wrapped in an old blue cloak, with coarse worsted stockings and one rusty spur; his head covered with a huge cauliflower wig, and a small cocked hat overtopping all'.

One of Parr's final acts of protest was as chaplain to George IV's estranged wife, Queen Caroline. It was officially decreed that prayer should be offered not for 'the King and Queen', but for 'the King and all the royal family'. Though Parr read what was prescribed by his sovereign, he circumvented the matter by inserting Caroline's name in another prayer instead which the authorities had overlooked.

Walter Savage Landor looked upon Parr as a father figure and on Parr's house as a second home. In an epitaph Landor wrote:

Here lies our honest friend Sam Parr:
A better man than most men are.
So learned, he could well dispense
Sometimes with merely common sense:
So voluble, so eloquent,
You little heeded what he meant:
So generous, he could spare a word
To throw at Warburton or Hurd:
So loving, every village maid
Sought his caresses, tho' afraid.

But Samuel Parr chose to be remembered in his little parish as one who had humbly served it for nearly forty years. The mural tablet in Hatton church pays tribute to the man 'who for 39 years was resident and officiating Minister of this Parish... Christian Reader! What doth the Lord require of you but to do justice, to love mercy, to be in charity with your neighbours, to reverence your holy Redeemer, and to walk humbly with your God?'.

— 8 —

The Peace That Never Was

ON 6 August 1814 the *Warwick and Warwickshire Advertiser* reported on a 'Grand Fete at Warwick' held on the racecourse two days previously, for which handbills from the organizers had requested 'each person to come provided with a Knife and Fork, Plate and Mug; as there would be much difficulty in procuring them for so large a number of persons they hope to see assembled on this happy and glorious occasion'.

This fête took place to celebrate 'The Peace That Never Was', or rather 'The Peace That Was Premature'. Napoleon was defeated in 1814, but the Peace Congress of Vienna was rudely interrupted in 1815 by the 'blip' of Napoleon's escape from exile in Elba, the Hundred Days and the Battle of Waterloo. Europe had already been celebrating peace the previous year after more than twenty years of almost continuous warfare, and this peace had been greeted nowhere more rapturously than in Warwick on the occasion of its victory fête.

'Amongst the various rejoicings,' reported the paper, 'to which the Peace has given birth, in almost every village and town in the empire, none, perhaps, have exceeded those which took place here on Thursday last. The predominance of joy over every other passion was never more truly evinced than on this auspicious day. Rich and poor, old and young, united in one gratulatory acclamation, and hailed the return of Peace with songs of triumph and gladness.'

The proceedings began at midday when a discharge of cannon announced the start of a carnival procession. When the procession finally reached the racecourse about 2 p.m. dinner was announced by a band playing 'Oh, the Roast Beef of Old England', and 'a very neat and suitable grace was said by the Rev. Arthur Wade, peculiarly appropriate to the occasion' - one would like to have known the exact words offered up by this unconventional clergyman! (See Chapter 10.)

The feast appears to have been of gargantuan proportions. There were twelve tables, each 120 yards in length; the quantity of beef

PUBLIC ENTERTAINMENT,
In Celebration of Peace.

The inhabitants of all descriptions in this Borough, *(Men, Women, and Children,)* are hereby invited to Dine together on the RACE-GROUND, on *Thursday*, the 4th of August next, at 2 o'Clock, to commemorate the restoration of *Peace* throughout Europe.

The Committee appointed to manage this undertaking, request each person to come provided with a *Knife and Fork, Plate, and Mug;* as there would be much difficulty in procuring them for so large a number of persons they hope to see assembled on this happy and glorious occasion.

Warwick, 25th July, 1814.

Printed at the Shakespeare Press, by W. Perry, Warwick.

Handbill of 1814 advertising the grand fête at Warwick.

weighed over 6,300 lbs; and there was a ton-and-a-half of plum pudding into which nearly 2,000 eggs had gone. 'Butts of stingo [slang for strong ale or beer in allusion to the sharp taste] flowed in every quarter, and it is supposed that between 4 and 5,000 gallons were drunk in the course of the day.' 'It is calculated that no less than 6,000 persons sat down to dinner, under the canopy of heaven', including about 300 Dragoon Guards.

There followed numerous toasts, among others for 'the King', 'the Heroes who fought and bled for the deliverance of Europe', 'the Duke of Wellington and our brave and gallant army', 'the Invincible Navy', 'the Land we live in', and (interestingly for so recent a conversion to the idea) 'the Abolition of Slavery all over the world'.

After this there was dancing, and the snooty reporter conceded that 'it is but justice to say that the populace of the lower classes conducted themselves with a degree of propriety which rendered them no unpleasant companions to the more polished part of the community, with whom on this festive occasion they so familiarly mingled'.

Amusements included two donkey races, a grinning match, and a sack race which was won by a one-legged sailor and which was enlivened by flour having been surreptitiously placed in the sacks beforehand. About 10 p.m. 'the day closed, as it commenced, with harmony and good humour' - except for a fight between two drunken coachmen who lost their coats and their fares while their fisticuffs were in progress. The newspaper estimated that between 12,000 and 15,000 people had attended the celebrations in the fine weather.

There were no such celebrations after the Battle of Waterloo the following year!

— 9 —

Was It Worth the Strife?

WALTER SAVAGE LANDOR may appear in anthologies, but few people today are familiar with the writer or his output. Yet he lived to the age of eighty-nine to become one of the longest-lived of great English writers. A contemporary of Wordsworth, a friend of Southey, he survived to become the friend of Dickens and Browning too, and was admired by the young Swinburne, who wrote that Landor 'had won for himself such a double crown of glory in verse and in prose as has been worn by no other Englishman but Milton'.

Landor was born in Warwick in 1775 in a house by the East Gate now called Landor House and part of the King's High School for Girls. He was the son of a relatively wealthy Dr Walter Landor, who came from Rugeley in Staffordshire, and his second wife Elizabeth Savage of Bishops Tachbrook near Leamington, where her family owned considerable property.

Like Wordsworth, Landor began life as a radical, but, unlike Wordsworth, continued so to the end - though paradoxically he does not seem to have seen any inconsistency between advocating left-wing views and living a life at times both aimless and luxurious on his independent means.

At the tender age of four-and-a-half he was sent to a boarding school at Knowle, near Solihull, and then before he was nine to Rugby School. Here he showed great promise in Latin, but eventually his father was asked to remove him after he had insulted the headmaster on two occasions. At eighteen he went up to Trinity College, Oxford, as rebellious and hot-tempered as ever, but the following year the 'mad Jacobin' was sent down for firing a shotgun at the window of a Tory undergraduate. The upshot was that he quarrelled with his father and left home, though this did not stop Landor senior making his son an allowance of £150, quite a sum of money in those days.

His temper and arrogance and inability to stand contradiction had early manifested themselves. Though kind and generous in many respects, and indignant more because of injustice than on personal grounds, his temper made him many enemies, even of one-time friends. Two men, however, whose friendship he retained to the end

Landor House, Warwick.

were Robert Southey, the Poet Laureate, and Samuel Parr, the eccentric vicar of nearby Hatton.

Landor was probably the author of an anonymous tract entitled 'The Dun Cow' written in defence of Samuel Parr in answer to another anonymous tract, 'Guy's Porridge Pot', lampooning his mentor. Both titles are evocative of old Warwickshire.

A bachelor till the age of thirty-six, Landor was nevertheless very much a ladies' man: two of his early loves figure in poems addressed to them - Nancy Jones as Ione and Jane Swift as Ianthe. Another name linked with his was that of Rose Aylmer whom he commemorated in his most popular short poems:

> Rose Aylmer, whom these wakeful eyes
> May weep but never see,
> A night of memories and of sighs
> I consecrate to thee.

In another youthful adventure, Landor went to Spain as a volunteer when the Spaniards revolted against Napoleon, but he was back in England before the defeat of Sir John Moore at Corunna early the following year.

In 1808 Landor bought the large estate of the ruined Llanthony Priory in the Vale of Ewyas beneath the Black Mountains in the Welsh Marches, with the intention of becoming a model landowner. Enthusiastically he set about landscaping the area, planting trees, improving roads, and importing Merino sheep. Money was no object – until it ran out – but the scheme failed because the ferocious temper of their new landlord antagonized the local peasantry and even an English tenant he had imported. On one occasion Landor is said to have been thrown from a first-floor window! No doubt there were faults on both sides. After five years of intermittent residence Landor left Llanthony for good in 1813.

It was to Llanthony that Landor had brought his bride two years before. At Bath in the spring of 1811 he had remarked of a girl at a ball, 'That's the nicest girl in the room. I'll marry her'. Two months later he and seventeen-year-old Julia Thuillier, a girl half his age, were married. Julia bore Walter four children, but it was an unhappy marriage – no wonder, when he later admitted, 'I married to get rid of love'. They went abroad, first to France and then to Italy where they lived much of the time in Florence. But a final quarrel with his wife in 1835 led him to leave her and the family in Italy and to return to this country where he settled in Bath.

It was during his exile that Landor produced his best-known work, *Imaginary Conversations,* about eighty discourses on all manner of subjects between pairs of people, both historical and contemporary – Milton and Marvell, Washington and Franklin, Henry VIII and Anne Boleyn, and, in our own field, Lord Brooke and Sir Philip Sidney. To these, other *Conversations* were later added, making nearly 150 in all. To the years after his return to England, which were punctuated by occasional visits to Warwick, belong *Examination of Shakespeare* (1834), *Pentameron* (1837) and *Collected Works* published in 1846.

In 1858 a libel action drove Landor back to Italy when he was over eighty years of age. The reunion between husband and wife was brief: Robert Browning found him first a cottage in Siena and then an apartment in Florence, where he died in September 1864 in his ninetieth year.

Some years before his death Landor wrote:

> I strove with none, for none was worth my strife,
> Nature I loved, and, next to Nature, Art;
> I warmed both hands before the fire of Life;
> It sinks, and I am ready to depart.

Yet his cantankerous temper had made his life one of disagreement and strife with all manner of people!

— 10 —

Fighter for the Working Class

T ODAY clergymen are castigated by politicians for meddling in politics, at any rate if they are left of centre. But it is not exactly a new phenomenon. Long ago the Warwick area produced two notable examples: first Samuel Parr and then the even more radical Dr Arthur Savage Wade, who was Vicar of St Nicholas, Warwick, from 1811 until his death in 1845. Wade was to absent himself from his parish for the last thirteen years of his life and become the champion of the working class.

A native Warwickian, he was born in 1787, the son of Charles Gregory Wade, the leader of the Tory party which controlled Warwick Corporation, and his wife Susanna Savage. He was a critic of the Church of England from within, and very tolerant of other Churches; he was a disciple of Samuel Parr and a friend of Dissent, of local Unitarians William Field and John and William Parkes. During the 1820s he was active in local progressive politics, and in 1827 he published a pamphlet in favour of Roman Catholic Emancipation. He took an active part locally in the Reform Bill election of 1831.

Shortly afterwards, seeking to labour in a wider field, Wade disappeared from local Warwick politics. Perhaps some clues to the direction in which he was heading can be gleaned from the title page of a published sermon which he preached at St Nicholas on 19 August 1832: 'A Voice from the Church: or a Sermon (with a few notes and amplifications) on Church Reform; pledges - cheap government - cheap justice - cheap food - cheap knowledge - and on a cheap and efficient medium of exchange; also, on the duties which the electors and elected will owe to the represented and unrepresented people of Great Britain and Ireland, especially to the working classes.'

Wade's two most important concerns were to be the Tolpuddle Martyrs and the Chartists. But he first became active in the Birmingham Political Union. When he then went to London he was originally connected with the Co-operative Movement and later with the National Union of the Working Classes. He spoke against flogging in the army and navy, and in favour of a free press - against 'taxes on knowledge', in particular the newspaper stamp duty. These campaigns drew Wade away from his Whig-Radical position as a disciple of Parr and made him the protagonist of working-class political demands. He chaired a meeting to set up the Midland Union of the Working Class - which was looked at askance by his middle-class colleagues in the Birmingham Political Union - and he denounced the Reform Act as too narrow and attacked the iniquitous new Poor Law.

However, as T. H. Lloyd has pointed out in his article on 'Dr Wade and the Working Class', our reforming cleric is

> best remembered for the prominent part which he played in the campaign of protest which followed the sentence of the Tolpuddle Martyrs [to transportation to Australia]. He chaired the meeting of the Grand National Consolidated Trades Union which initiated the London campaign, marched 'in full canonicals' in the great procession from the Copenhagen Fields on 21 April [1834] and was among the deputation which waited on Lord Melbourne to present the national petition calling for clemency for the Martyrs. Melbourne's rejection of the petition was not the end of the matter, and Wade continued to be associated with the campaign for the return of the Dorchester men. When that campaign was successful he played a prominent part in the march and dinner held to celebrate their return.

Finally Arthur Wade espoused Chartism, with its six points of universal suffrage, the secret ballot, the abolition of property qualifications for M.P.s, the payment of M.P.s, equal electoral districts and annual parliaments. (All but the last, which is considered impracticable, have been achieved today.) The proceedings of the People's Convention which assembled on 4 February 1839 began with a prayer by Dr Wade, afterwards printed for distribution: 'Grant, O God of Nations, that the folly or perverseness of our rulers may no longer deprive the poor of the comforts of life, nor deny to Thy people any of the social or political rights... We beseech Thy blessing upon all moral means for obtaining our political and social improvement, be evermore our ruler and guide, that we may so pass through things temporal that we lose not things eternal.' Note the words 'all moral means': he sided with the 'moral force' party, and retired from the Convention when the 'physical force' Chartists got the upper hand.

What of his position as Vicar of St Nicholas? In December 1833 he had been granted permission to be non-resident in his parish on medical grounds. These appear to have been real enough: he suffered from apoplexy. But as has been pointed out, 'the illness does not seem to have interfered much with his political activities, and it is difficult to believe that the excitement of these, coupled with the fogs of London, could have had a more therapeutic effect than a quiet life in Warwick'.

In May 1834 Wade was forbidden to preach, probably because he had accepted the post of chaplain to the London trade unions. When we think of the value of industrial chaplains today, this hardly seems to be a grave offence! But writing at the time, the Editor of *The Times* took a quite different view:

> We suppose that his Diocesan thinks he may do less harm in London than in the parish of St Nicholas. He, poor half-witted gentleman, is scarcely worth a thought. We suppose some friend looks after him, to see that he does 'not walk into a wall', where he might happen to stray, in the hope of finding truth, or the other half of his wits.

When in 1836 Wade proposed to return to his parish, he was repulsed by the parishioners: the curate in charge wrote to the bishop, 'I felt it my duty to tell Dr Wade very decidedly that it was the full determination of his parishioners to prevent his return by every means in their power'.

A controversial character indeed! Whether you think he should have resigned his living or not – he paid for a curate, but kept the title of vicar – there is no doubt that he was a very practical Christian. But when a willow tree was planted in St Nicholas churchyard in his memory on 24 November 1934, at the time of the centenary of the Tolpuddle Martyrs, it was not the clergyman who was remembered, but the man who, in the words of the accompanying tablet, 'fought for the freedom of all workers'.

— 11 —

Warwickshire's First V.C.

T HE Victoria Cross is our highest decoration for 'bravery in the presence of the enemy'. A plain bronze Maltese cross on a crimson ribbon, it is superscribed 'For Valour'. It was instituted by Queen Victoria in 1856, but some awards were made retrospectively, so that when the Queen held the first investiture the following year, recipients included heroes of the Crimean War as well as of the Indian Mutiny. Indeed, the medals were appropriately cast from the metal of Russian guns captured at Sebastopol.

One such hero of the Crimean War was Lieutenant Frederick Miller of the Royal Artillery who was awarded the Cross in May 1859 for bravery at the Battle of Inkerman which was fought outside Sebastopol on 5 November 1854. Miller lived at Radway Grange, near Edgehill, where King and Parliament had fought the first pitched battle of the Civil War over two hundred years before.

In the Battle of Inkerman the British and French troops defeated the Russians in a series of hand-to-hand encounters. Miller's citation told of his 'having at the Battle of Inkerman personally attacked three Russians and, with the gunners of his division, prevented the Russians from doing mischief to the guns which they had surrounded'. He had previously called for assistance from part of a retreating infantry regiment, but when this was denied him, Miller and his few men laid about them with swords and rammers; one man was a boxer and felled several of the enemy with his fists.

Frederick Miller rose to the rank of Lieutenant-Colonel, and died in Cape Town in 1874 when still only forty-two years of age. He and his two brothers, who also died abroad, are commemorated on the grave of their father – soldiers, all four of them – in what was the churchyard of the building which preceded the present Victorian church in Radway. The father, Lieutenant-Colonel Fiennes Sanderson Miller, is commemorated by an obelisk in the Edgehill woodlands: he commanded the Sixth Inniskilling Dragoons at the Battle of Waterloo, and for his bravery during the action, in which he was severely wounded, he was made a Companion of the Order of the Bath.

Lieutenant-Colonel Frederick Miller, V.C., of Radway.

Frederick's great-grandfather was the gifted eighteenth-century amateur architect Sanderson Miller, the squire of Radway. He built the folly tower on Edgehill on the spot where King Charles I had raised his standard before the battle, and he was also the architect of the Shire Hall in Northgate Street, Warwick.

The family was distantly related to the Fiennes family of Lord Saye and Sele of Broughton Castle just over the border in Oxfordshire – hence the use of Fiennes as a Christian name. Unfortunately the male line died out – there was said to be a curse on Frederick's family – and the Millers' two-hundred-year ownership of the Radway estate came to an end in 1916. But Radway's military tradition, exemplified by Frederick and his father, continued when Field-Marshal Earl Haig came to stay with his sister, the new tenant at Radway Grange.

— 12 —

Shepheard's Hotel

I N Eathorpe, a village just off the Fosse Way a few miles from Leamington, a number of houses bear the inscriptions 'S.S. 1860' and 'S.S. 1861'. They refer to Samuel Shepheard, the founder of Shepheard's Hotel in Cairo.

Shepheard's was well known to Middle Eastern travellers for a hundred years. It was opened in 1851 as a staging-post on the route to India and rebuilt in the 1890s on a grander scale. It became so popular with the great and famous that its visitors' book had to be chained down. Anyone who was anyone was to be seen on the terrace drinking four o'clock tea. Over the years its guest list included Anthony Trollope, Sir Richard Burton and General Gordon, Queen Marie of Romania and King Leopold of Belgium, King Alfonso of Spain and Winston Churchill. Its bar was frequented by generations of British troops on active service, and especially by headquarters staff, derisively named the 'Short Range Shepheard's Group' or the 'Chairborne Division'. The bartender, Joe, served concoctions called the Dying Bastard and the Dead Bastard, and the hotel's popularity with officers during the Second World War occasioned the following doggerel:

> We fought the war in Shepheard's and the Continental Bar,
> We reserved our punch for the Turf Club lunch
> And they gave us the Africa Star.

Romantic tales of Middle East intrigue were woven about the hotel in spy and thriller books and films.

The Warwickshire man from whom the hotel takes its name was only a boy when his parents died. Samuel Shepheard was apprenticed to a pastry cook by his uncle with whom he lived at the Crown Inn, Leamington. He ran away to sea, but as a steward on a liner he supported some mutineers and was discharged in Egypt with only a shilling in his pocket. However, he prospered and became manager of the British Hotel in Cairo before he was thirty. A few years later he acquired an old palace from the Egyptian Pasha and proceeded to convert it into the hotel ever afterwards known as Shepheard's. He was a tough businessman, and an American traveller described him as 'a short, sturdy, strongly-built John Bull of the old type, both in looks and manner, independent and brusque to the very verge of rudeness and often beyond; no respecter of position or of persons, yet full of geniality and generous impulses, concealing a heart of gold under a rough husk'.

He continued to prosper in wartime as well as in times of peace. He obtained a contract to victual the troops passing through from India to the war in the Crimea, and later he supplied the troops being sent in the opposite direction to suppress the Indian Mutiny. On one occasion when the officers of a certain regiment did not pay their mess bills, he followed them all the way to the Crimea and obtained his money in the trenches before Sebastopol!

After nine years he sold the hotel in 1860 for £10,000, a very large sum of money in those days. He retired to Warwickshire where he had purchased Eathorpe Hall and became the village squire and the chairman of the parish council. Here he built those houses for the villagers and also a bridge over the River Leam where there had only been a ford before.

Alas, his role as benevolent lord of the manor was not to last long. He died at the early age of fifty in June 1866: perhaps the strain of overwork, which his meteoric rise to riches must have involved, had taken its toll. He is buried in nearby Wappenbury churchyard with his wife and a ten-year-old daughter, in whose memory a grieving mother presented the organ to the church. A tablet in the church records four more children who died in infancy and are interred in the British Protestant burial ground in Cairo. Three daughters survived but, to his deep disappointment, no son and heir.

Sadly Shepheard's Hotel is no more: it was destroyed by fire by a Cairo mob in 1952, signalling the beginning of the Egyptian revolution and the end of colonialism. A new hotel perpetuating the name was opened on another site in 1957, but it failed to recapture the grandeur of the old.

— 13 —

'Half a league, half a league, half a league onward'

GEORGE and Maria Garnham gave a glimmer of hope to the inmates of Warwick Workhouse. They needed it. The Poor Law Amendment Act of 1834 had meant the refusal of outdoor relief to the able-bodied poor, and as result had rendered inadequate the town's small workhouses in St Mary's parish in the Saltisford and in St Nicholas in Coten End where the Millwright Arms now stands. A bigger workhouse had to be built for the new Board of Guardians of the Warwick Union of thirty-five parishes which included Leamington and Kenilworth and the surrounding villages. It was opened in 1839 to accommodate paupers, variously estimated at between 200 and 355, and was situated in Union Road, otherwise Packmore Lane, now Lakin Road. The austere, spartan workhouse, later to be called The Institution, and finally Lakin House, was described at the time as 'a handsome building of red brick, in the Elizabethan style of architecture'. A workhouse infirmary was built in 1849 on the opposite side of the road - later it was the nucleus of the hospital - and a chapel was built next to the workhouse in 1884.

The conditions of the workhouse were fortunately tempered by the kindness of George Garnham and his wife Maria, who were appointed Master and Matron in 1865. As a trooper, Garnham was a survivor of the Charge of the Light Brigade, that courageous but forlorn charge ordered by incompetent generals into the mouths of the Russian guns in the Crimea in 1854. Somehow he had escaped without injury, but his horse had been shot under him and he had returned to the British lines on foot. Subsequently he had endured the tremendous privations which the British soldiers went through the following winter in the Crimea. He was evidently not so seriously affected as to need the ministrations of Florence Nightingale in Scutari, but back home he was invalided out of the army with rheumatism and with the rank of sergeant. On recovery, he became successively an employee of the Great Eastern Railway, a warder at Dartmoor Prison and a workhouse master in County Durham. Then he came to Warwick, where both he and his wife cared for the unfortunate poor for nearly thirty-five years.

Sadly, when Maria Garnham was compelled to give up her appointment as Matron because of ill-health, George had to resign too, because the appointment was a joint one. This weighed heavily on his mind, and after showing his successor the ropes, he committed suicide on the day of his retirement by drowning himself in the canal near the workhouse. *The Warwick and Warwickshire Advertiser* of 3 March 1900 speaks of 'a long record of conscientious service, in which the deceased outlived many boards of guardians and gave them all complete satisfaction . . . He considered the children in the Workhouse the special object of his care'. It was also noted that at the time of his death George Garnham was a director of the Warwick Building Society, a sign both of his involvement in the life of the town and of his high standing in the community.

A plaque was placed in the workhouse chapel. Under the Crimea Medal with Balaclava bar was the inscription:

> In grateful recognition of the faithful services rendered to this Union by Mr. George Garnham, late of the 13th Light Dragoons, who rose with that regiment as one of the illustrious 600 in the ever memorable Balaclava charge, under General the Earl of Cardigan, K.G., on the 25th October 1854. Thus he served his Queen and country, and upon his retirement from the Army was Master in this House for 35 years. This brass is erected to his memory by many of the Guardians and officers of this Union. He died Feb. 28th, 1900. Aged 64 years. 'The Lord grant unto him that he may find mercy with the Lord, in that day'.

Why that particular text? A commentary on the Victorian attitude to suicide? On demolition of the chapel, the plaque was fortunately saved, and is now in the keeping of the 13th/18th Royal Hussars Headquarters at York.

Another survivor of the Charge of the Light Brigade was Troop Sergeant Major, later Regimental Sergeant Major, Seth Bond, a native of Southam. He was decorated three times, once for his humanity in sparing a Russian soldier who had wounded him. He died at the age of eighty in 1902 and is buried in Southam churchyard. In addition, a third survivor, Job Allwood, lived in Leamington.

— 14 —

'Who is on the Lord's side?'

WHO will serve the King?' A different kind of soldier is referred to in this hymn by Frances Ridley Havergal, who was also the author of such hymns as 'Take my life and let it be Consecrated, Lord, to Thee,' and 'Master, speak, Thy servant heareth'. One of her favourite metaphors in describing the role of the Christian was that of the soldier, and this particular battle-hymn refers to the story of the captains of the tribes of Israel in I Chronicles 12 giving their allegiance to David after Saul's death in battle.

But why include Frances Ridley Havergal? Because she lived in Leamington for some years. She was born in 1836, the daughter of a Worcestershire clergyman, Canon William Henry Havergal, who was successively Rector of Astley, near Stourport; St Nicholas, Worcester; and Shareshill, between Cannock and Wolverhampton. Frances never married. She was often unwell, and she was prevented by the constraints of the society of her day from pursuing a career. When Canon Havergal retired in 1867, they (father, stepmother and Frances) bought a newly built semi-detached house in Binswood Avenue in Leamington. They named the house Pyrmont Villa in memory of the place that had become their favourite continental health resort. Today it is plain 43 Binswood Avenue.

Frances travelled widely both at home and abroad, to relatives and friends, and for health, holiday or missioning (mainly through music but also speaking and writing), so that she must have been away from Leamington for considerable periods. However, she became increasingly involved in church affairs in the town. She had regular commitments to the Leamington branch of the Y.W.C.A. and local branches of missionary societies. She was much in demand for her musical services. For example, the Revd Thomas Bromley invited her to sing to an assembly of 500 poor people at his annual Christmas party at St Mary's in south Leamington, and on another occasion she gave an evening recital of sacred music to the patients at Leamington Hydropathic (the Pump Room). Her biographer tells us, however, that Frances set most store on her training of the choir of St Paul's Church in the north of the town:

In view of the congregation, which she describes as 'a really first-class one, both as to size and social position' [a touch of snobbery here, perhaps?] she felt that the choir had a particularly demanding task if they were not merely to lead the singing, but at the same time to be an effective instrument for evangelisation. Her own role, she believed, was to equip them for this, both by insisting on high musical standards, and also enabling them to deepen then own spiritual lives.

And yet, sad to record, partly because of temperamental difficulties with her stepmother, Frances Ridley Havergal never seems to have been quite at home in the house in Binswood Avenue in which she officially lived for eleven years. And it was not until the Revd Joseph Rogers of St Paul's told her that 'he had never in his ministry been so distinctly conscious of receiving help, blessing and influence from another', that she realized that her contribution to the spiritual life of Leamington was far greater than she had imagined.

On the death of her stepmother in 1878, Frances left Leamington for South Wales where she died of peritonitis a year later at the age of forty-three.

— 15 —

Farm Labourers'
Champion

T HE march of progress in rural areas has been slower than that in the towns, whether it be mains electricity, piped water or living conditions generally. Nowhere was this more evident than in the case of the agricultural labourer whose plight in the mid nineteenth century was far worse than that of his fellow worker in the town. The farm worker lived in appalling conditions in a tied cottage on perhaps ten or eleven shillings a week. Until, that is, the visit of two Wellesbourne men to a Barford cottage to see a certain Joseph Arch on 7 February 1872.

Joseph and Mary Pace, the grandparents of this Joseph Arch, had been servants at Warwick Castle, living in one of the lodges there. Their wages were augmented by the coppers tossed to them by the gentry for opening the lodge gates. When they had saved enough money they bought a cottage in Barford, three miles away, in 1794 for the princely sum of £35. Not long after they had moved into the tiny cottage opposite the parish church their daughter Hannah left home to enter service at the Castle in her turn. She married one of the coachmen there, and on his death took as her second husband John Arch, a native of Rowington, north-west of Warwick. When Joseph Pace died, John and Hannah Arch moved in to live with Hannah's widowed mother, and in this cottage Joseph Arch, the youngest of four children, was born on 10 November 1826.

Joseph inherited an independent spirit from his strong-willed mother, and, though he had to leave school at the age of nine, he was an omnivorous reader whose self-education was remarkably successful. His first job at that tender age was as a crow-scarer at fourpence for a twelve-hour day. After a year of this, he obtained work as a ploughboy at three shillings a week. By the time of his marriage at the age of twenty in 1847 to Mary Ann Mills, a domestic servant from nearby Wellesbourne, he was earning about eleven shillings a week. But with a growing family - he was to have seven children, all but one of whom

The cottage in Barford in which Joseph Arch lived for most of his life.

survived childhood - this was not enough. So having become some-thing of a labouring all-rounder - he could not only plough but could turn his hand to carpentry and also won several prizes at agricultural shows for hedging and ditching - he decided to go freelance and do contract work for any farmer who would hire him for a specific job. This meant that he would journey throughout the Midlands and even into South Wales, often sleeping rough, in order to earn more money to support his family.

Joseph Arch had joined the Primitive Methodists and had become one of their local preachers, and he would preach when on his journeys as well as when he was at home. Also on his journeyings he saw much of the plight of his fellow rural labourers. So he was ready when the 'call' came - his own word, his speeches being naturally filled with Scriptural language - and he accepted the invitation of those two men who called on him to address a meeting of farm labourers at Wellesbourne that evening. The room booked at the local public house was far too small for the great number of labourers who turned up (between 500 and 600), so the meeting was held outside on the green under a chestnut tree. Some opponent had seen to it that the lamps had not been lit, but the men provided their own lanterns. Standing on an old pig-killing stool, Joseph addressed the men as 'children of Israel waiting for some-one to lead them out of the land of Egypt' - and he obviously saw him-self as their Moses. He advocated the setting up of a union (there had recently been sporadic attempts to form agricultural unions else-where) and that evening it was agreed to form a committee and a depu-tation to meet their employers.

A week later (14 February 1872) a larger meeting some one thousand strong met on the same village green. Again Arch was the principal speaker. He called for a daily wage of three shillings and a nine-hour working day, and a union was formed there and then. He also tramped from village to village addressing many other meetings. When the local farmers rejected their demands, 200 workers in Wellesbourne and the neighbouring villages went on strike. The employers responded with lockouts and threats of eviction from tied cottages (Arch was at least fortunate in owning his cottage), but money flooded in from well-wishers and the strike gained national publicity. The result was reason-ably successful: many workers gained wage increases, though others migrated to better jobs in the urban north, and yet others emigrated. This was not a solution Arch favoured until he was invited to Canada the following year to see for himself and negotiate more favourable conditions, and even then he always regarded emigration as a secon-dary solution to the main one of higher wages.

Meanwhile events proceeded rapidly. A few weeks later, on Good Friday, 29 March, a meeting was held in the Portland Street public hall in Leamington in which all the local branches were formed into a War-wickshire Agricultural Labourers' Union. The committee appointed Arch as Organizing Secretary at 21 shillings a week. Then two months later, on 29 May, the National Agricultural Labourers' Union came into being - again in Leamington (the meeting was held in the newly com-pleted Circus, a large wooden hippodrome near the Pump Room), such was the strength of the movement in Warwickshire itself. Half the sixty or so delegates to that meeting were local preachers like Joseph Arch, an indication of the debt which the new union owed to Methodism. A national headquarters was established in Leamington and Joseph Arch was elected President at £2 a week with a roving commission to spread the word up and down the country.

Unfortunately, N.A.L.U. was never as successful as in its earliest days. From a peak of 86,000 members in 1874 it had declined to 20,000 by 1880 and probably had only a thousand members when it was wound up in 1896. This was partly due to improvements in conditions, but also partly due to internal wrangling within the union over alleged mis-management of finances, for which Arch was not responsible, and over centralized control, for which he was. Those who wanted a loose federation of local unions regarded him as a dictator, but Arch rightly believed that only a strong centralized union could be an effective in-strument in improving the conditions of farm labourers.

Until the mid 1880s Joseph Arch devoted himself mainly to union activities, but he was also interested in political action on the Liberal side as a means of improving the lot of farm workers. Urban workers, or rather the male householders among them, had got the vote in the Second Reform Act of 1867. Arch wanted the rural workers to have it too. They got it with the Third Reform Act of 1884. By now the secret ballot had been established, and Arch urged the labourers to use their newly won franchise as a further means of improving their lot.

Joseph Arch himself was the first agricultural labourer to become a Member of Parliament. He served as Liberal M.P. for North-West Norfolk from 1885 to 1886 (he lost his seat by a mere twenty votes when the Liberal party split over Home Rule) and from 1892 to 1900, and in between he served as a member of the original Warwickshire County Council from 1889 to 1892. In 1898 he published his autobiography which was prefaced and edited by his friend Frances Evelyn, Countess of Warwick. She actually brought the Prince of Wales to visit the old man in his cottage on one occasion; Arch, with some pride, regarded the Prince as his constituent because Sandringham lay within his constituency.

These years, however, were something of an anti-climax. He had entered Parliament too late in life. True, he spoke in the House on six occasions during his first short experience there. But during his second spell from 1892 to 1900 he made only twelve speeches, and none at all after the end of May 1894 - 'Drinking his bottle of whisky a day, but hardly opening his mouth for any other purpose', as one trade union history unkindly puts it. Indeed, the one-time Primitive Methodist and teetotaller, who retired to Barford and died on 12 February 1919 at the age of ninety-two in the house in which he was born, does seem to have been corrupted to some degree by the changes in his life-style.

Nevertheless, more than any other man in the nineteenth century, Joseph Arch stirred the national conscience on behalf of his own class. The ochre-washed cottage in which he had lived most of his life still stands. A public house in Barford has been named after him. In Barford churchyard a granite obelisk stands by his grave, erected in 1922 by the National Union of Agricultural Workers (successor to the N.A.L.U.) 'in appreciation of services rendered to the agricultural workers of the country. His soul goes marching on'. And in Wellesbourne, though the original chestnut tree died in 1948, the spot is marked by a stone, and a replacement tree has been given to the village, a commemorative plaque recording the story. Moreover, since 1980 an annual commemoration service has been held in Wellesbourne Methodist Church under the auspices of Luton Industrial College and the agricultural workers' group of the Transport and General Workers' Union.

The memory of a fighter for his fellow men lives on.

— 16 —

Anyone for Tennis?

REAL Tennis, or Royal Tennis, or, simply and more correctly, just Tennis, has been played for centuries. Two hundred years ago, at the beginning of the French Revolution the Third Estate withdrew to a tennis court to take the famous Tennis Court Oath not to disperse until they had given France a constitution. Long before that we have Henry VIII building the Royal Court at Hampton Court Palace, and Shakespeare's Henry V (in Act I, scene ii) being sent a present of tennis balls as an insult by the Dauphin. The game was played indoors, but only by a privileged few. Incidentally, south Warwickshire can boast of having two of the few remaining real tennis courts in the country at Leamington and Moreton Morrell.

If, however, the game was played outdoors, an expensive special-purpose building would not be required. With this in mind, Major Harry Gem, a Birmingham solicitor, and his friend Augurio Pereira, a Spanish merchant, experimented in 1860 with a type of lawn tennis which they called pelota. In 1872 both men moved to Leamington, Gem to Arran Lodge, 5 Hamilton Terrace and Pereira to 33 Avenue Road, now Abacroft Rest Home. With two doctors from the Warneford Hospital, Frederic Haynes and Arthur Wellesley Tomkins, they teamed up to form a Lawn Tennis club, the world's first, in the summer of 1872. They played a game of lawn rackets, as they called it, on the lawns of the Manor House Hotel almost opposite Pereira's home, the court area now being occupied by Manor Court flats. Another major, Clopton Wingfield, publicized and marketed the game, and the All England Croquet Club in Wimbledon codified the rules.

On the occasion of the centenary celebrations in June 1972, a plaque was erected on the front lawn of the Manor House Hotel: 'In 1872 Major Harry Gem and his friend Mr J. B. A. Pereira joined with Dr Frederic Haynes and Dr A. Wellesley Tomkins to found the first lawn tennis club in the world, and played the game on nearby lawns'. And another plaque was erected at the same time in Hamilton Terrace, close to the corner of the police station: 'Major Harry Gem lived in a house on this site from 1872 until his death in 1881. In 1872 he

The first lawn tennis club: a sketch by Harry Gem.

foundedinLeamington the first lawn tennis club in the world and was its first President'.

The first men's singles champion at Wimbledon, in 1877, was Spencer W. Gore, brother of the first Bishop of Birmingham. Twins William and Ernest Renshaw, of Brandon Lodge, Brandon Parade, Leamington (now 60 Holly Walk), dominated Wimbledon in the 1880s. William won the men's singles six times in a row (1881-6), an all-time record, and they won the doubles together on seven occasions.

The first Wimbledon ladies' singles champion also came from Warwickshire. Born at Harrow in October 1864, Maud Watson was the daughter of the Revd Henry William Watson, assistant mathematics master at Harrow School. They moved to Warwickshire the following year when her father became Rector of Berkswell. She learned to play tennis on the rectory lawn mainly against Cambridge undergraduates who were studying mathematics with her father. After doubles successes in Leamington tournaments in 1882 and 1883, Maud won the first ladies' singles title at Wimbledon on 20 July 1884, at the age of nineteen, defeating her sister Lilian 6-8, 6-3, 6-3. She died in June 1946 at the age of eighty-one and is buried with her sister in Berkswell churchyard. The centenary of her triumph was celebrated in 1984 in period costume in the garden of Well House, formerly Berkswell Rectory.

Much more recently another Warwickshire woman has won the ladies' singles. After being a losing semi-finalist five times and the beaten finalist in 1967, Ann Haydon Jones of Birmingham defeated Billie Jean King to take the Wimbledon title in 1969. In the same championship she also took her second mixed doubles title.

Recently there have been few British successes, but Jeremy Bates of Solihull came within match point of reaching the quarter-finals of the men's singles in 1992.

— 17 —

Sea Fever

I must go down to the seas again, to the lonely sea and the sky,
And all I ask is a tall ship and a star to steer her by,
And the wheel's kick and the wind's song and the white sail's shaking,
And a grey mist on the sea's face and a grey dawn breaking.

JOHN MASEFIELD, Poet Laureate for thirty-seven years, yearned for the sea. Born at Ledbury in Herefordshire in 1878, he was sent to Warwick School as a boarder before he was ten years old. 'I was wretched at first,' wrote Masefield looking back. 'I was too young. And they found I wrote poetry. I tried to kill myself once by eating laurel leaves, but only gave myself a horrible headache. Once I ran away, and was brought back by a policeman and flogged.' However, the following year a junior house was opened for the smaller boys, 'so that they might be under a milder regime by themselves'. He enjoyed the rest of his time there – he stayed until he was twelve – made friends easily, and liked cricket, gymnastics and swimming. He later wrote, 'It was a good school, the masters were a fine lot, and the place had a high tone'.

He entered the merchant service at the age of thirteen: he served his apprenticeship on a windjammer and acquired that intimate knowledge of the sea which gave atmosphere and authenticity to his work. Unfortunately he was forced ashore through ill health. After three years in New York, he returned to England in 1897, making his mark first as a journalist. He was to write novels and plays, naval histories and children's books, but he was outstanding as a poet. Pieces such as 'Salt Water Ballads' are evocative of the sea, and 'Reynard the Fox' illustrates his other love, the country-side. One of his finest prose works was *The Nine Days Wonder* in which he saluted the men who achieved the miracle of Dunkirk. In all these works a sympathy for the defeated and the persecuted emerged.

Warwick School early this century.

Masefield was Poet Laureate from 1930 until his death in 1967, and was awarded the Order of Merit in 1935. His life and his writings had been dedicated to helping the weak against the strong. This dedication must undoubtedly have been influenced not only by the rigours of the sea, but also by the harshness of boarding-school life in Warwick.

— 18 —

Father and Daughter: Writers Extraordinary

MANY people would probably opt for Barbara Cartland if they were asked to name our most prolific woman author. But while she has indeed written over 520 books to date, she still has some way to go before overtaking Warwickshire's Ursula Bloom, who had some 560 to her name when she died in 1984 at the age of ninety-one. The fiction shelves of the library may not contain many titles under her own name, but that is because she not only also wrote non-fiction, but used a variety of pseudonyms - Sheila Burns, Mary Essex, Rachel Harvey and, most intriguing of all, Lozania Prole, a name coined by her publisher Charles Eade, 'lozania' being Spanish for 'blossom' or 'bloom' and 'prole' Spanish for 'seed', a play on his own name, C. Eade!

Ursula is well known as a writer. What is not so well known is that she inherited her talent and stamina for writing from her father, the Revd James Harvey Bloom, who achieved a considerable reputation as a scholar and an antiquarian. After several curacies up and down the country - at Hertford, Harwich, Hemsworth and Chelmsford - and some teaching in Warwickshire at Long Marston, he served as Rector of Whitchurch, south of Stratford, from 1895 to 1917, a tiny parish of some 120 souls, with its church only approachable over fields, a living in the gift of the Roberts-Wests of nearby Alscot Park. A likeable fellow with a shock of red hair and unbounded energy, he declined preferment, partly because he was concerned with the care of his flock, materially as well as spiritually, and partly because the smallness of his parish allowed him to pursue his researches in genealogy and natural history. He was never happier than when rummaging around old deeds or registers, churchyards or the countryside. The eccentric writer Marie Corelli, who lived at Mason Croft in Stratford, introduced him to Methuen's who published his book *Shakespeare's Church*, and to Unwin's who published *Shakespeare's Garden* in which he listed every flower mentioned by Shakespeare. Frances Evelyn, Countess of Warwick, got him to help her with research on her two-volume work *Warwick Castle and its Earls*. Harvey also edited the first volume of the *Victoria County History of Warwickshire*, he produced books on the history, geography and folklore of the county, and he catalogued the cathedral libraries of Worcester, Hereford and Rochester.

Although he followed the social convention of employing a number of servants in his sprawling rectory in spite of his modest stipend, Harvey did not necessarily kow-tow to the high and mighty, or even to those who felt they deserved it. A trivial incident involving Ursula developed into a wholesale row with the imperious Corelli. The ten-year-old girl, borrowed by Marie to attend her at a flower show, innocently asked her at lunch in front of the other guests if she was divorced (she wasn't - it was servants' gossip that Ursula had overheard). In a rage Marie immediately took Ursula home to demand an explanation from Harvey, and when she found her parents were out for the afternoon, took it upon herself to assemble the Bloom servants and cross-examine them! On his return Harvey was justifiably annoyed: he supported his daughter, but kept his temper. A series of letters passed between Bloom and Corelli, each one more uncompromising than the last. Then Marie Corelli wrote an account of the incident in a Birmingham newspaper. Harvey responded by writing to a London paper. He was perhaps fortunate not to be involved in a court case, because Marie had a predilection for issuing writs. (On another occasion she sued a writer to the *Stratford Herald* for libel and was awarded a farthing's damages: the next day the editor was deluged with masses of the coins from well-wishers!) But this time she did not invoke the law: the Bloom-Corelli row just simmered on throughout the winter.

The following Spring, 1903, Marie Corelli published a guide book to the Stratford Festival for American tourists called *The Avon Star*. Alas for her, she was not an historian and the book contained a number of inaccuracies. An enterprising printer contrived to obtain an advance copy and persuaded Harvey at a moment's notice to burn the midnight oil and produce a counter-blast. And so, also on Shakespeare's birthday, out came *The Errors of the Avon Star*, at sixpence half the price of the original. Marie's book began with 'Murmurings of the Avon', Harvey's with 'The Gurglings of the Brook', and so on. On that birthday night performance, Harvey was cheered as he entered the Memorial Theatre, people waving their copies of his green booklet which they had brought with them. Marie enquired about the cheering as she arrived, and promptly turned round and went home in another rage. The play that night was *The Winter's Tale*. For Marie it was winter! In revenge she proceeded to lampoon Harvey as the clerical villain in her next novel *God's Good Man*. Harvey found all this very amusing. It is said that the day after Marie's humiliation her companion happened to pass him in

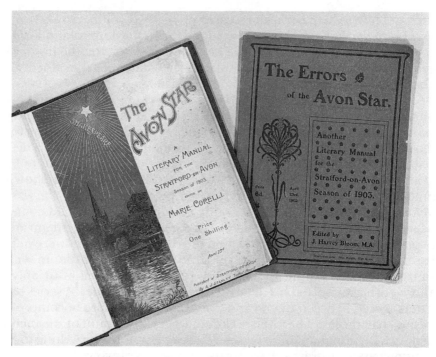

The Avon Star, *and Harvey Bloom's riposte.*

the street: she put out her tongue at him, but Harvey responded by raising his hat, and said afterwards, 'I hope I did the right thing'.

Unfortunately, and particularly for a clergyman, Harvey had a weakness: he was very much a ladies' man, a flirt. It was all very innocent on his part, and he thought nothing of it, but some of the ladies concerned took him seriously, and it got him into a number of awkward situations. Indeed, when his wife Polly died, there were two ladies who expected to become the second Mrs Bloom! Matters came to a head some years earlier when Harvey went to Weston-super-Mare to convalesce after an illness. There he met two maiden ladies, Miss Sims and Miss Birch. He showered his charm on Josephine Sims, and Miss Birch in a fit of pique reported the matter to Jo's brother, an alderman of Bath, with whom Jo lived. He told his sister she must give up her friendship with this married clergyman or leave the family home. She asked for time and appealed to Harvey. Ever the gallant gentleman, he went to see the alderman and tried to explain things to him, but that only made matters worse. The interview developed into a confrontation, Jo was thrown out, and Harvey had to find her lodgings.

Nor did fortune favour Harvey at home. Polly found out about this difficulty of his quite accidentally. Funerals are rare in a parish of only

120 souls, but unexpectedly the heat wave killed an elderly labourer in a Whitchurch harvest field. Assuming he was away cataloguing cathedral documents, Polly sent a telegram to Worcester requiring Harvey's immediate return. At the last minute she had to get a neighbouring clergyman to officiate, and when Harvey returned from Bath two days later and had to explain to his wife, he proceeded to drop an even bigger brick. It would convince that stupid alderman that there was nothing in it if Polly invited Jo to spend a fortnight at Whitchurch with the family. Polly would have none of it! She told Harvey to drop the whole thing, but he wouldn't.

More flirtations followed, and Harvey also continued his contact with Jo (he had to find her a job, for instance). Eventually Polly, a sick woman, had had enough. In 1909 she and Ursula left Whitchurch to move into lodgings in Stratford, in the hope that their absence would make Harvey see sense. Unfortunately it did not. In fact he installed Jo as housekeeper. The bishop hinted that if he was to retain the living Mrs Bloom must come back, but when Harvey went to see his wife and daughter at Walton-on-the-Naze whither they had moved, he expected them to return without his dismissing Jo! Mrs Bloom refused, but the bishop, who was a good friend of Harvey's, did nothing. And when in March 1917 Polly died of cancer, Harvey didn't even attend the funeral, merely noting in his diary, 'My wife died today. I went to tea with Scarlett Potter [another local historian] and saw some most interesting seals'.

Ursula warned her father not to remarry, telling him that if he did so she would take action to prevent his new wife from living in the Warwickshire rectory his first wife had loved so dearly. Yet only a few weeks after Polly's death, in early May, he and Jo were married at Whitchurch. However vindictive it may seem, we can understand Ursula's action in reporting the whole matter to the bishop, who could then no longer turn a blind eye to his friend's indiscretions. A fortnight later Harvey left for ever the parish in Shakespeare country to whose needs he had ministered for over twenty years.

Meanwhile Ursula had had enough problems of her own. In childhood she had suffered from a gangrenous ankle which troubled her all her life. As a teenager she had had to listen to some of her father's confidences, and then bottle them up so as not to repeat them to her mother. Then she had to look after an invalid mother and earn some money to keep them both by playing the piano at a local cinema as accompaniment to the silent films of the day. In 1916 she married Captain Arthur Denham-Cookes, but within two years, weakened by drink, he succumbed to the infamous influenza epidemic of 1918, leaving her with a baby son to care for.

Her urge to write never abated, but during her brief marriage she had to destroy each manuscript as she finished it because Arthur detested her writing books. After the war she got into Fleet Street. She also

Ursula Bloom.

began to sell her books, became one of the first 'agony aunts' and was appointed chief crime reporter on the *Empire News* and the *Sunday Dispatch*, tracking down Ethel le Neve, Crippen's mistress, who had gone into hiding after his execution. In 1925 she became a naval officer's wife, marrying her beloved 'Robbie', Commander Charles Gower Robinson. But she continued writing her books, besides copious contributions to the *Sunday Pictorial, Woman's Own* and *Home Notes* – all this in spite of a chronic migraine for which she had several operations.

Father and daughter met intermittently, for Harvey had set up in High Holborn as 'Archivist and Genealogist' and was in and out of the British Museum, the College of Heralds, Somerset House and the Society of Genealogists. But when war came again Ursula brought her father and his wife away from the air raids and found them somewhere to live in Stratford. He got a job at the Shakespeare Birthplace Trust, sorting valuable deeds brought there for storage during hostilities, and transcribing the parish registers of south Warwickshire and the adjacent areas of Worcestershire and Gloucestershire. He hated waste-paper pulping for the war effort, but he was overjoyed to discover and rescue from destruction both a valuable first edition and a deed signed by Elizabeth I. It was after a long hot spell tramping the streets of Stratford searching paper salvage in hope of further treasures that he had a stroke. Within a few days, in May 1944, the old man whom people called Sunny Jim died in the town he loved so well. He is commemorated by a memorial in his church at Whitchurch – a wooden plaque carved with oak leaves.

Ursula and her husband lived in Chelsea after the war, and she went on writing, averaging ten books a year. Not by any means were all her books light romances, either. She also wrote biographies, historical fiction and family sagas. *Parson Extraordinary* is an affectionate but critical and sometimes bitter portrait of her father, who was also *The Elegant Edwardian* who ministered to *The Changed Village.* She continued writing until after her ninetieth birthday and died the following year in a Hampshire nursing home. Through all her tribulations it was her writing which kept her going. The book she wrote about her life as a writer, *The Mightier Sword,* ends with the words, 'Without my pen I could not have lived'.

— 19 —

Mutton Dressed as Lamb

ND what of the good lady who tangled with Harvey Bloom? Almost forgotten and little read today, Marie Corelli in her day was the most sensational of bestselling novelists, a legendary figure second only in renown to Queen Victoria, whose favourite author she was claimed to be. *The Sorrows of Satan* sold more copies than any previous English novel, in spite of her refusal to send any copies for review. And it was this formidable lady who set about impressing her stamp upon Stratford-upon-Avon, with either the approval or the disgust of the townspeople - for she was a character whom people either loved or hated.

Marie was born Mary Mackay in London in 1855, though she was invariably called Minnie. She was probably the illegitimate daughter of Charles Mackay, editor of the *Illustrated London News*, and Mary Elizabeth Mills, whom he subsequently married after the death of his first wife. Such circumstances at that time caused Marie to be suitably vague about her parentage.

She was already achieving fame as a romantic novelist when she first visited Stratford in 1890 - her first novel, *A Romance of Two Worlds* four years before, had been an immediate success - and in 1899 she came to live in the town, briefly at Hall's Croft, once the home of Shakespeare's son-in-law Dr Hall, and eventually at Mason Croft in Church Street, now the Shakespeare Institute of Birmingham University, where she remained until her death.

You could say that Marie Corelli's whole life was a deception - or perhaps it would be more accurate and more charitable to describe it as fantasy, because she deceived herself, or at any rate tried to deceive herself, as much as anyone. Claiming modesty, she sought notoriety. Professing contempt for society, she was eager to be part of it. (Did she never realize that she was invited to dinner parties as an eccentric?) Coming to Stratford at the age of forty-four, she claimed that she was not yet thirty and dressed as a teenage girl. She continued to lie about her age, resolutely refusing to be photographed, and when she finally had an 'official' photograph included

Marie Corelli with her ponies.

as a frontispiece to one of her novels, it was touched up to make the fifty-one-year-old look about thirty!

What infuriated her opponents was her vanity. Yet to her it was not vanity. She was the voice of conscience – she was always right, she knew the truth so she had to speak out. And her exotic and colourful stories – usually with herself as heroine – forever moralizing, and with good always triumphing over evil, appealed to her public for that very reason – no matter how the critics slated her. It didn't even matter that her novels contained descriptive inaccuracies which could not be attributed to artistic licence. As one of her biographers remarks, 'She appointed herself the guardian of the public conscience . . . Had there been a Viewers' and Listeners' Association in her day, Miss Corelli would certainly have been its President'.

Nevertheless, on arrival in Stratford she sought to be pleasant to the townspeople. Only five weeks after her arrival she wrote to the Headmaster of the Grammar School offering to take the whole school to the circus as her personal treat. But as her biographer points out, 'It was a magnanimous gesture, but it was symptomatic of the tactlessness which bedevilled Marie that she did not wait rather longer before wishing to bestow the benefits of her presence on the town. It looked as if she was trying to "take over" '.

But if she was enamoured with the idea of herself as a great writer coming to live in the town of another great writer, she did have a real concern for Stratford. She was successful in preventing a large memorial to a relatively minor actress from overshadowing the memorial to Shakespeare in Holy Trinity Church. Her brushes with Harvey Bloom and the *Stratford Herald* were part of a wider campaign to prevent the demolition of old properties adjacent to Shakespeare's birthplace in Henley Street. And later she was instrumental in rescuing from neglect Harvard House, the home of the mother of the founder of the American university. If only Marie had not been such a tactless egotist, refusing to concede any virtue in the proposals of her opponents, she would not have made so many enemies among the local worthies!

Marie Corelli also drew attention to herself through two unusual modes of transport. She and her companion, Bertha Vyver, would go out for a daily ride in a toy cart drawn with difficulty by two tiny Shetland ponies, 'Puck' and 'Ariel'. Later she imported a full-size gondola from Venice, complete with an Italian gondolier, and Marie and Bertha were rowed in state up and down the River Avon. Unfortunately the Italian frequently got drunk and incapable, and had to be dismissed. One of her gardeners had then to dress up in the gondolier's costume and deputize! *Punch* accordingly published a limerick:

> There was a fair siren of Strat.,
> Who narrated the Sorrows of Sat.,
> She's a gond. on the Av.,
> She was everyone's fav.,
> Though she used Shake's Trustees as a mat.

And an enterprising Stratford newsagent, tongue in cheek, published a series of six somewhat amusing coloured postcards purporting to show Marie in her gondola, in her pony-chaise and so on. She sued him for libel, and her solicitors sent threatening letters forcing the local shops to withdraw them from sale. The judge, however, dismissed the case. Nevertheless, the supply of postcards dwindled rapidly – Marie may have bought them up and destroyed them. At any rate, they are now collectors' items.

The eccentric lady died in 1924 and lies in a prominent angelic grave in the local cemetery on the Evesham Road.

— 20 —

The Polar Connection

BEFORE he set out for the South Pole in 1910 Captain Robert Falcon Scott and his wife Kathleen spent some of his last few days in England at Binton, near Stratford, in the rectory home (now a private house) of her brother, Revd Lloyd Bruce. And in St Peter's Church in the village there is now a magnificent memorial west window to that famous expedition.

The four-light window is divided into compartments by stone mullions, and across the centre run four panels with text below each, telling the story of the ill-fated expedition. The first light depicts Scott and his companions saying farewell in high spirits; the second shows the party reaching the South Pole in January 1912 to find Amundsen's flag already planted there; in the third scene Captain Oates goes out into the blizzard to die, so as not to be a burden to his friends; and the final picture shows the search party erecting a cairn eight months later to mark the last resting place of Captain Scott, Dr Wilson and Lieutenant Bowers. In the tracery at the top of the window can be seen a picture of the mast of the ship the *Terra Nova* and a further sight of the memorial cairn. Surmounting all is a picture of the Crucifixion and the text 'Greater Love hath no man than this'. There is also a tiny scriptural scene at the foot of each compartment.

The glass came from the workshops of Messrs Kempe, and one of the craftsmen, John W. Kubler, has recorded, 'Among the very many windows on which I worked during my 24 years in the Kempe Studios, few, if any, gave me greater pleasure, as an artist and craftsman, than the creation of the Scott memorial. I well remember working on the sketch designs and cartoons'.

Mrs Scott, a talented sculptor, was the youngest of eleven children of the Revd Stewart Bruce, Canon of York. Ten years younger than her husband, she met Scott at a tea party where one of the guests was J. M. Barrie. They married in September 1908 in the chapel at Hampton Court. Their son, Peter Markham Scott (Sir Peter Scott, the naturalist), who was born in September 1909, was named Peter after Peter Pan, and Markham after Sir Clements Markham, President of the

Panels from the Scott window in Binton Church.

Royal Geographical Society. The boy was only three, and staying with his grandmother Hannah Scott, when the telegram arrived with the news that Scott and his party had perished on their return journey from the Pole. His mother did not hear the news until nine days later. She was sailing to New Zealand to meet her husband there on his return.

Scott was posthumously knighted, and his wife was granted the same rank and precedence as if he had lived. She sculpted a statue of him for Portsmouth Dockyard, and another stands in Waterloo Place, London. She also sculpted a marble figure of him for Christchurch, New Zealand, and for Cheltenham, where Dr Edward Wilson was born, she created a statue of the doctor wearing sledging clothes. But surely the most impressive monument is the window in the tiny Warwickshire village church.

Warwickshire can boast two other polar explorers - Wally Herbert of Welford-on-Avon who reached the North Pole on 6 April 1969, and Frederick George Jackson of Alcester (1860-1938) after whom part of the Franz Joseph Land archipelago, at 85 degrees north, is named.

— 21 —

The Better 'Ole

C ARTOONISTS from Hogarth to Giles have provided perfect contemporary social commentary. A few great cartoons have become pieces of history - 'The Curate's Egg' and 'Dropping the Pilot', for instance - but none more so than 'The Better 'Ole' of Warwickshire's Bruce Bairnsfather.

Bruce was born in July 1887 in Indian hill country near Rawalpindi where his father was a serving army officer. He was sent back to England to a minor public school at Westward Ho! in Devon. Eventually his parents returned to this country, and in 1904 they transferred him as a weekly boarder to Trinity College, Stratford, so that he could be put through a cramming course for entering the army, which it was automatically assumed would be his career, despite the fact that he displayed a great flair for drawing at an early age. His parents moved to be near him and rented half of the large Spa House at Bishopton, just outside Stratford, which dated from 1837 when an abortive attempt to develop a health resort to rival Leamington Spa was planned for the village. It still stands today, one half the Victoria Spa Lodge guest house, the other a private residence, appropriately named Bruce Lodge.

Attending an evening art class at the newly built Stratford Technical College, Bruce Bairnsfather became its star pupil. Tom Holte, the Headmaster of the Art School, quickly recognized his special talent. Bruce even drew on the college's lavatory wall some sketches which clearly displayed features that were to be characteristic of Old Bill ten years later: fortunately the sketches were photographed when the lavatory was pulled down twenty-five years later.

In 1905 Bruce joined the 3rd Militia Battalion of the Royal Warwickshire Regiment at Budbrooke Barracks, outside Warwick. He was commissioned in the Cheshire Regiment, but he did not find army life congenial and resigned two years later, intent on an artistic career. He went to London and enrolled in the John Hassall School of Art near Earls Court but, not being able to make a living as an artist, he took a job as an electrical apprentice with the firm of Spenser's in Henley Street, Stratford, founded by Spenser Flower of the brewing family. He pro-

"Well, if you knows of a better 'ole, go to it."

Bairnsfather's famous cartoon.

gressed to become a lighting engineer for large country houses, and finally a sort of speciality salesman to the gentry. But all the while the artistic side in him was pleading to come out. The ubiquitous Marie Corelli took him under her wing, and he had advertisement designs accepted by such firms as Players, Liptons and Beechams. He was a natural actor, too. The family put on annual Christmas amateur dramatics, converting the Great Bath Room of Spa House into a miniature concert hall for the villagers of Bishopton. He often appeared at these concerts in drag. He also performed in pantomimes at Compton Verney, the home of Lord Willoughby de Broke.

Bruce volunteered at the outbreak of war, was commissioned into the 3rd (Reserve) Battalion of the Royal Warwickshires, and in November 1914 went to France with the 1st Battalion, in which both 'Monty' and A. A. Milne also served. He was involved in the famous unofficial Christmas truce that winter, when British and German frontline troops fraternized in No-Man's-Land. In April 1915 he was invalided home with shell shock. Meanwhile he had sent his first war cartoon – 'Where did that one go to?', with the shell exploding on top of the dug-out – to *The Bystander* magazine, a copy of which he had happened to see lying around at the time. It was accepted. There followed 'They've evidently seen me,' a shell whizzing through the base of the chimney-stack in which a look-out was perilously perched. Convalescing in hospital, Bruce was asked to do a weekly drawing. 'That 16 inch Sensation' was the next – a shell aiming straight for the poor soldier whose legs are shackled by immense balls and chains as he tries to escape. All were drawn from personal experience, and gradually the figure of Old Bill evolved. Finally, in October 1915, came the classic 'Well, if you knows of a better 'ole, go to it'. This led to the popular *Fragments from France*, with 'The Better 'Ole' on the cover, and a number of other memorable cartoons included: 'Keeping His Hand in' – the juggler practising with hand grenades; 'The Same Moon' – the girl at home romantic at the thought that the same moon is shining down on her man, and the soldier in No-Man's-Land cursing it for its brightness; 'Mice' – the reply of the old sweat as to who made the large shell hole in the wall; and 'Staying at the Farm' – writing home against a background of wrecked farmhouse and dead animals. *Fragments* was followed by *More Fragments, Still More Fragments* and other sequels, nine in all. As early as September 1916 Old Bill and his mates Bert and Alf had appeared in a five-minute sketch in the revue *Flying Colours*. Before the war ended, 'The Better 'Ole' had been made into both a musical play (written by Bruce) and a silent film; he had written a book, *Bullets and Billets*; and postcards and pottery alike teemed with Bairnsfather motifs.

Ordinary soldiers and civilians took to Old Bill. But, as Bairnsfather's biographers point out:

> The Army staff could not accept … the comparative inadequacy of carefully planned official propaganda campaigns – often because some of the cartoons poked gentle fun at them!…[Old Bill, Bert and Alf] coped with everything the enemy, their N.C.O.s, their officers or The Staff could throw at them. People loved their honest roguery

and their apparent ability to carry on their own lives despite the efforts of enemy or authority to challenge them. Bill, Bert and Alf were the soldiers of reality, scruffy and comfortable. That wasn't the image that the authorities had of their soldiers. It wasn't the image that most senior officers welcomed in their headquarters, well behind the lines. The Blimps soon began to carp at Bairnsfather's work.

But the French asked for him to be loaned to them. The War Office agreed, and in the one solitary act of recognition British officialdom ever conceded to him, he was appointed 'Officer Cartoonist' in the Intelligence Department. And so he became very popular with French, Italian and American troops as well.

In a sense, the rest of Bairnsfather's life was a bit of an anti-climax. He must have seemed a voice from the past when he died at the age of seventy-two in September 1959. However, he remained immensely popular in the immediate post-war years. He continued to draw, paint, write, lecture and act on both sides of the Atlantic. He ran his own *Fragments* magazine for fifteen months during 1919 and 1920, and contributors included Heath Robinson and Studdert-Kennedy. He initiated the Old Bill Fraternity in aid of St Dunstan's for blinded servicemen. Another play, *Old Bill M.P.*, appeared in 1922 and a second *Better 'Ole* film in 1926. Bruce left Bishopton in 1919, purchasing Waldridge Manor near Princes Risborough in Buckinghamshire, where he had his own miniature theatre. Unfortunately, however, he made an unhappy marriage: his wife had a bad temper and a drink problem, and belonged to a fast-spending, socializing jet-set which the essentially shy Bruce did not get along with. Though now, despite his lack of business sense, he periodically made a lot of money, he tended to have plenty of cash one minute and be almost bankrupt the next: indeed, at one point bankruptcy proceedings were started against him. The downward trend began in 1928 when *Carry On, Sergeant!*, a film he himself directed in Canada, was a flop. For the rest of his life he seemed listlessly to move from house to house in an almost nomadic existence.

He had limited success again in the Second World War, when his artistic skills were put to good use not only for Britain but also as official cartoonist to the American forces in Europe: his *trompes l'oeil* on murals were so convincing that on one occasion a visiting general ordered a lifelike painting of a slouching G.I. to be reprimanded! But Bairnsfather never really broke the stranglehold of Old Bill. That character made people lose sight of the fact that he was also a gifted painter. He was greatly disappointed when in 1945 an oil painting which he submitted to the Royal Academy was turned down. Nevertheless, today Bairnsfather items are eagerly sought as collectables, and if you want to indulge in a little nostalgia, you can see some of his original sketches in the Royal Warwickshire Regimental Museum in St John's House, Warwick.

— 22 —

A Countess on the Hustings

F RANCES EVELYN, Countess of Warwick, is famous as the great society belle and hostess of the 1890s, and 'Darling Daisy', the mistress of the Prince of Wales. What is not so well known is that in later years she became an ardent, if untypical, Socialist. Her biographer Margaret Blunden writes:

> The impression she would have made on first acquaintance was paradoxical: charming but autocratic as a hostess, progressive in outlook but dated in manner, radical as ever in politics but at all times a grand, imperious figure and full of gossip about high society, she was unpredictable, an enigma some found intimidating.

As the journalist R. D. Blumenfield put it, 'She is Comrade Warwick to the proletariat, but around the comradeship she hedges herself with an aura of dignity and aloofness which bodes ill to the zealot who dares to address her as "Comrade". She is always "Your Ladyship"; invariably the Grande Dame'.

The General Election of December 1923 produced what today we would call a hung Parliament: the Conservatives, though still the largest party, lost their overall majority and were defeated on an Amendment to the Address, and Labour as the second largest party formed their first minority government with Liberal support. However, in such circumstances there were many Labour candidates who had not been elected, one of these being the candidate for Warwick and Leamington, Lady Warwick, now in her sixties.

In fact it all started off as a by-election caused by the resignation of the sitting Conservative member. Now it was indeed a courageous act on the part of Frances to embark on a pioneer struggle to try to win for Labour the very area she had once dominated as a society hostess, with most of her relations and friends supporting her Conservative opponent. In their eyes, for her to have stood for Labour anywhere else would

65

Frances Evelyn, Countess of Warwick.

have been bad enough, but to stand in Warwick was the height of bad taste. It was also highly embarrassing that her Conservative opponent should be her daughter-in-law's brother, a young war hero, Captain Anthony Eden, M.C. Moreover, Eden had just become engaged to the step-daughter of Lady Warwick's own daughter. The Edens were close friends of the American tenant then in residence at Warwick Castle (Frances was living at Easton Lodge in Essex at this time), and her son sent a public letter to his brother-in-law giving him his support. No wonder the Press had a field day!

Tempers became frayed. Then, during the campaign, Parliament was dissolved and the by-election was cancelled to be merged into the ensuing General Election. Frances struggled on, although the strain of what became the longest ever campaign in British electoral history inevitably told on her stamina. Arthur Henderson, George Lansbury and Beatrice Webb all came to speak on her behalf. *The Times* reporter commented:

> I saw one of these open-air meetings in progress in Covent Garden Market [the area in Leamington behind Tesco now occupied by a multi-storey car park], not a particularly salubrious part of the town. Perhaps it was not typical, but it was highly diverting. The Countess was supported by several "comrades" and was listened to for the most part by wondering children. There were a few adults.

On the other hand the *Daily Herald* reported that at one of her crowded meetings a 'typical working woman' seized Frances by the shoulder, crying, 'You don't want bouquets, you want votes and you shall have them'. Lady Warwick battled on, and on the eve of poll addressed nine meetings throughout the constituency. But in the event Eden was returned with over 16,000 votes, the Liberal candidate came second with over 11,000, and Lady Warwick trailed a poor third with only 4,015. With hindsight it was not surprising. Interest had been mistaken for support. The public had been sympathetic or indulgent or merely amused, but they would not take her candidature seriously. A few months later she failed to get elected even to her local council in Essex. And when another General Election was called ten months later, she refused to stand again.

— 23 —

Massacre on the Road to Dunkirk

T HE miracle of Dunkirk was the result of a number of factors: the calm seas; the heroic actions of the little boats coming to the rescue; the German concentration on their main drive towards Paris; the foolishness of Hitler in halting the Panzers in order to give the egotistical Goering the chance of destroying the British Expeditionary Force with the Luftwaffe alone; and finally, bad weather which temporarily grounded the German planes. But the miracle was also due in no small part to self-sacrificing rearguard actions, including the heroic stand of men from the Second Battalion of the Royal Warwickshire Regiment on 28 May 1940 at Wormhout, a few miles inland. Here they inflicted heavy casualties on the enemy before being obliged to surrender. Unfortunately for them, the enemy was not the ordinary Wehrmacht, but units of Sepp Dietrich's notorious Waffen S.S. Fit and injured men alike were brutally marched some way from the village to a meadow in the hamlet of Esquelbecq, the captors kicking, clubbing and bayoneting stragglers on the way. Up to one hundred men (the exact number will never be known) of the Warwickshires, the Cheshires and the Royal Artillery were then herded into a small barn which was hardly large enough to hold them all.

The S.S. then proceeded to lob grenades into the barn, causing several casualties. One of the bombs was smothered by the heroic action of a C.S.M. and a sergeant throwing themselves upon it and being immediately killed. The only officer among them dragged a wounded private away as the Germans themselves took cover from the explosions of the grenades: he saved the other man's life, but was killed himself. After the last grenade had been thrown, the Germans ordered five men outside and shot them. Five more were ordered outside: they were also shot, though one of them miraculously survived. Yet another five were ordered out, but this time there was a stubborn refusal. The guards conferred. At this point there was a torrential downpour. The murderers had no desire to become drenched as they dealt out death, so they stormed into the barn. The men near the entrance were ordered to turn round and were shot in the back: again, one actually survived. Moving further into the barn, the Germans trampled on the dead and wounded, opening fire with automatic weapons. After that they pre-cipitately left.

This heinous massacre was made worse by being a botched-up job: many of the British soldiers were left wounded and dying. It is impossible to say exactly how many were killed, but it was probably about 85. Iden-tity discs had been removed from nearly every prisoner shortly after capture: this would appear to indicate that the massacre was premedi-tated. Moreover, when the German authorities discovered the reason for the existence of so many bodies in a mass grave, they were anxious to disperse them, and reinterred the majority in other locations. As a result today only thirty of the victims lie in the Military Cemetery at Esquelbecq. There were fifteen known survivors - either uninjured men who got out of the barn and were later captured (one, unfortu-nately, was shot evading capture), or injured survivors who were more kindly treated by other Germans when the barn was cleared. Several are still alive today.

It has never been established who was responsible for ordering the massacre. Dietrich, the S.S. general, was sheltering in a ditch at the time, pinned down by British fire. Revd Leslie Aitken has meticulously researched the story in his *Massacre on the Road to Dunkirk*. A certain S.S. office, Wilhelm Mohnke, then the battalion commander and later a trusted general in Hitler's Berlin bunker, has been linked to the affair. He is still alive in Hamburg, but he has never been brought to trial and the possibility of a cover-up exists. Ian Sayer and Douglas Botting, in their recent book *Hitler's Last General*, claim that sufficient evidence exists for Mohnke to stand trial for this and for several other atrocities.

— 24 —

Operation Anthropoid

OPERATION Sealion, Operation Barbarossa and Operation Overlord are all well-known code names of the Second World War. But what was Operation Anthropoid? It was the secret Czechoslovak plan to assassinate Reinhard Heydrich who, despite his youth, was Himmler's S.S. deputy and head of the S.D., one of the most powerful men in Hitler's Germany. He was also the organizer who set up the extermination machinery which led to the deaths of six million Jews. Our story begins, however, when Heydrich was appointed so-called 'Protector' of Bohemia and Moravia on 27 September 1941 and began an unparalleled reign of terror over the Czechs. This was so extreme that President Benes, in exile in Britain, reluctantly sanctioned a plan to kill him despite the certainty of reprisals. The Czechs were already committing internal acts of sabotage and go-slow against German war production factories in their homeland, but Benes was concerned that his countrymen, who had been betrayed at Munich and over-run without a shot being fired, should make a more direct and spectacular contribution to the Allied war effort from outside. What followed has been well told by Alan Burgess in *Seven Men at Daybreak* and Callum MacDonald in *The Killing of S.S. Obergruppenfuhrer Reinhard Heydrich.*

The Czech patriots assigned to kill Heydrich came from an infantry company based at Moreton Hall, now the county's college of agriculture. Indeed, the Czech government in exile occupied part of the Compton Verney estate and its fine house, and 3,000 men of the Czech Brigade were stationed from October 1940 onwards in Leamington and places nearby such as Moreton Morrell, Moreton Paddox, Wellesbourne and Kineton. The Brigade's headquarters were in Harrington House, since demolished, and several other buildings in Leamington's Newbold Terrace.

After secret intensive special training in Scotland with the Special Operations Executive, five Czechoslovak exiles were dropped over Bohemia under cover of darkness one cold December night in 1941. Two of them, Jan Kubis, a Czech, and Josef Gabcik, a Slovak, had been assigned to kill Heydrich. The mission was extremely hazardous. Problems multiplied from the start. The Halifax bomber dropped the parachutists seventy miles off course, and Gabcik injured a foot as he landed. Marked men, they had to avoid detection; they had to hide the arms dropped with them in a safe place; they had to convince their underground colleagues already there that they weren't German spies. Once in Prague, they eliminated one by one the methods of achieving their objective. The deadly unarmed combat in which they had been trained would be of no use because they could get nowhere near Heydrich, who was heavily guarded whether at home or at his headquarters, Hradcany Castle. Heydrich commuted from a villa fifteen miles outside Prague, but his chauffeur drove too fast for them to kill him by shooting. He often made journeys to Berlin by special train, and they managed to get details of these. However, detonating the line with explosive might kill the engine driver, but not necessarily all the passengers, or the one passenger in particular. They found that the train stopped briefly at a heavily guarded suburban station and they hid in trees some distance away, but even then the train accelerated away too quickly for them to identify Heydrich, let alone for them to be able to shoot accurately.

In the end they decided to ambush Heydrich on 27 May 1942, as he was being driven to Prague airport for Berlin, making use of a hairpin bend in the city where the car would have to slow down. As it happened, Josef's sten gun failed to fire because the safety catch stuck. Jan's hand grenade, intended to finish things off, hit the car moments later but, as they fled, they saw Heydrich get out – it seemed as if their mission had failed. In fact, the grenade had exploded splinters of steel from the car which penetrated deeply into the spleen and lumbar regions of Heydrich's back. Blood poisoning was to set in, and the Reichsprotector died in hospital eight days later, as painfully and slowly as many of his own victims had died.

It took some time for the Nazis to round up all those remotely connected with the assassination, but in the end Gestapo intelligence and torture, with the help of traitors who either cracked or wanted to save their own families, ran them all to earth, though not before Nazi ferocity in revenge had resulted in the execution of hundreds of people who had no connection whatsoever with the event. The last act was played out on the morning of 18 June when the S.S. surrounded the church of St Cyril and St Methodius where Jan, Josef and five others were hiding. After inflicting heavy casualties on the Germans, Jan was killed, and the other six turned their revolvers on themselves in order to avoid capture.

In the Jephson Gardens in Leamington, near the Jephson Temple, stands a Czech memorial, a large bronze plaque on a block of rough granite, facing on to a fountain, the top part of which is shaped as a parachute: a stream of water from the top falls down the grooves and

then into the open air to represent the cords of a parachute.
On this stone 'parachute' are
inscribed the names of the
members of the mission, described in the wording of the
plaque:

> In tribute to all Czechoslovak
> soldiers, airmen and patriots
> who fell in World War II.
> From Royal Leamington
> Spa, in 1941, volunteers
> from Free Czechoslovak
> Forces stationed in the town
> were parachuted into their
> homeland to rid it of the ty-
> rant "Protector", S.S. General
> Heydrich. Two of them – Jan
> Kubis and Josef Gabcik –
> accomplished their mission
> in May 1942. They and their
> companions laid down their
> lives for freedom.

*The Czech memorial in the Jephson
Gardens, Leamington.*

In a rose bed near the monu-
ment is a bronze plaque:
'Lidice shall live. Garden of Remembrance. 25th anniversary 1967'. The
Nazi revenge massacre at Lidice occurred on 10 June while Jan and
Josef were still on the run. 'In the course of the search for the murder-
ers of General Heydrich,' Nazi propaganda ran,

> it was ascertained that the population of this village [Lidice] sup-
> ported and assisted the perpetrators. Apart from the help given to
> them, the people also committed other hostile acts, such as the keep-
> ing of an illegal dump of munitions and arms, the maintenance of
> an illegal transmitter, and the hoarding of an extraordinarily large
> quantity of goods which are controlled.

All of this was patently untrue. No one in the village near Prague had
ever heard of Jan Kubis or Josef Gabcik, or had helped the resistance
in any way.

Nevertheless, all the men and lads over fifteen were taken from their
homes, lined up against the wall of a barn and shot. Their bodies were
buried in a mass grave nearby. All their womenfolk, 195 of them, and 95
children were piled into lorries and driven off to concentration camps
where most of the women died and most of the children were killed.

Eight children were considered fit for 'Germanization' and only sixteen children could be traced after the war. Workers on night shift were arrested on returning home, and shot. One man, sensing disaster, escaped into the forest, only to be betrayed later and also shot. Another Lidice resident was in hospital at the time, but when he had recovered he was shot too. In total 199 men were murdered, according to cold-blooded Gestapo records.

Not only that, the Nazis completed, in the fullest medieval sense of the word, the razing of the place to the ground. Bulldozers moved in to level the houses, and fleets of lorries transported the rubble away. It was intended to obliterate the village from the face of the earth. Shortly afterwards, a second lesser-known village, Lezaky, suffered the same fate as Lidice, and by the September of 1942 the Germans had murdered some three thousand Czechs.

The result was not what the Nazis had intended. The action did not cow or intimidate. Even in a war full of atrocities, the immediate reaction was one of enormous anger. It was almost unbelievable that even Hitler's regime should boast of such an act. A 'Lidice Shall Live' campaign was immediately launched. Coventry strongly supported it, and in 1946 the city was officially represented at the laying of the foundation stone of a new Lidice. When a rose garden scheme for the village was organized in 1954, Coventry sent a thousand rose trees from its Parks Department nurseries, and the city council has since been represented at other Lidice ceremonies. There is a plaque to Lidice just outside the shopping precinct. And in Czechoslovakia a new Lidice has arisen, adjacent to the site of the old which is now a vast empty space of remembrance.

In 1992, the fiftieth anniversary of Heydrich's assassination was commemorated at a ceremony in the Jephson Gardens, and special prayers were said in Coventry Cathedral for the people of Lidice.

If you have never heard of Operation Anthropoid, you will probably never have heard of Operation Reinhard either. That was the official name which the Nazis gave to the Holocaust in a macabre tribute to Reinhard Heydrich, the evil genius who had planned it all - before his assassination by Czech patriots based in Warwickshire.

— 25 —

Mr Vera Brittain

SIR George Catlin (1896-1979) is not perhaps a well-known name, but in his day he was an 'all-rounder' who rubbed shoulders with the greatest in the land. He was a prolific author on political, social and philosophical subjects. He was Professor of Politics at Cornell University from 1924 to 1935 and Professor of Political Science at McGill University, Montreal, from 1956 to 1960. He was high in the counsels of the Labour Party, and twice a parliamentary candidate. But his main concern was international relations: at various times he was a special foreign correspondent in Germany, in Russia, and in Spain at the time of the Civil War. He had been concerned with the policy of the Atlantic Community continuously since 1925. He was a joint founder of the America and British Commonwealth Association, now the English Speaking Union, and in 1970 he was knighted for his services to Anglo-American relations.

He also campaigned for Indian independence. Visiting India in 1947, he met Gandhi three times, once when the Mahatma was having his bath. He advised Mountbatten (Viceroy of India) that Gandhi would be favourable to the British plans if the Viceroy listened to what Gandhi had to say, even though it might take a long time. Later Mountbatten told Catlin, 'Well, I took your advice. It was quite true that we had to listen to the whole of his life story, but in the end we got the agreement we wanted'.

Sir George Catlin's fame has been eclipsed by that of his wife and daughter. In 1925 he married Vera Brittain, the author of *Testament of Youth* and *Testament of Experience*, the former being her First World War experiences which were so movingly portrayed on television. And his daughter is Shirley Williams.

And the local connection? His mother's family, the Ortons, came from Atherstone in north Warwickshire. Grandfather Richard Harding Orton was a jeweller in Leamington; he also invented a railway-brake, but unfortunately it proved uncompetitive to the Westinghouse brake which the railway companies adopted. His parents, Revd and Mrs George Catlin, lived before the First World War in Leam-

Memorial inscription to Sir George Catlin in Old Milverton churchyard.

ington, at 5 Church Terrace and then at 22 Church Hill. And Sir George himself was educated at Warwick School and became president of the Old Warwickians Association. His funeral took place at St Mary Immaculate Roman Catholic Church, Warwick, and he lies buried, a 'Scholar and a Gentle Man', in Old Milverton churchyard where Vera Brittain is also commemorated.

— 26 —

Industrial Troubleshooter

D O you remember the name of Sir Jack Scamp (1913-1977), the industrial troubleshooter of the 1960s? He lived at Ufton, the village between Leamington and Southam. Born in Birmingham, as a young man he was employed by the Great Western Railway. During the war he was invalided out of the Royal Artillery with a knee injury. From 1942 to 1944 he was assistant personnel manager with the Rover group, before becoming personnel manager with a Birmingham motor vehicle components firm for a year. For eight years he was personnel manager to the Rugby Portland Cement Company, and then he served from 1953 to 1958 as chief personnel officer with the Plessey organization. In 1958 he joined Massey Ferguson in Coventry and became director of personnel and industrial relations. There followed four years with G.E.C. and five with A.E.I., and finally in 1972 he became chairman of the management consultants Urwick, Orr & Partners of Rugby.

But it was during the years from 1964 to 1970, at the call of the Labour government, that Sir Jack's reputation grew as the country's leading industrial peacemaker, a role for which his background eminently fitted him. When Lord Devlin led an inquiry into the docks in 1964, Scamp was one of the four members of that committee. For a short while, from February 1965 to April 1966, he was seconded to the Department of Economic Affairs as Industrial Adviser, and was later honoured as Associate Professor of Industrial Relations at Warwick University from 1970 to 1975. He was chairman of the Motor Industry Joint Labour Council and conducted more than twenty inquiries within that industry. He also chaired inquiries into disputes affecting railway footplate staff, transporter drivers, aluminium castings workers, airline pilots, dockers, pressed steel workers, sewing machinists at Fords, shipyard workers at Barrow, coal trimmers and council workers. His efforts at conciliation were notably successful. But he remarked that his constant writing of reports which necessarily exposed skeletons in the cupboard would in the end make people say that they did not want to have him looking into their affairs again!

Indeed, such headlines as 'Jack Scamp blames both sides' became a newspaper commonplace.

He was rewarded with a knighthood and a deputy lieutenancy of Warwickshire. One industrialist wrote at the time of his death:

> If I had to describe in a single word the sort of man Jack Scamp was, the word which comes at once to mind is 'clean'... Uncorrupted by close contact with power in politics and the Trade Union movement, this quality made Jack trusted by everyone who had to do with him. More than that, his courtesy, unwillingness to think the worst of anybody, tolerance, good temper and good nature evoked extraordinarily widespread affection and respect.

We could do with more people like him at the present time.

— 27 —

Within Sound of Bow Bells

REVD Joseph McCulloch, the unconventional Rector of St Mary-le-Bow in the City of London during the 'sixties and 'seventies, had come to Warwick as Vicar of St Mary's Collegiate Church in 1949 after serving in parishes in Liverpool, Blackheath, Buckinghamshire, Essex and Chatham. His predecessor, the radio parson Canon W.H. Elliott, told him, 'The last five men have broken their hearts here'.

But McCulloch's heart did not break, and he stayed ten years. He was noted for his outspokenness and his pithy comments were often reported in the local press. He questioned whether even a tenth of what had been spoken about religion in the context of the Queen's Coronation was anything more than 'well-intentioned waffle'. 'On great national occasions,' the *Warwick Advertiser* reported him as saying, 'there is a widespread tendency to let religion out of the lumber-room in the form of a warm, pink smell. The air gets full of religious intentions. But beware of trying to pin this religiosity down to earth: I doubt if it will stay there.' In one of his many books, *My Affair with the Church*, McCulloch wrote:

> I have found it [the Church of England] a Church imprisoned and confused by its past, locked within outworn systems of thought and structure inhibiting that elasticity of mind and freedom of action upon which its effective ministry in the modern world depends. My affair with it has been a lifelong struggle to draw attention to the radical changes this precarious situation demands, and to bring the Church into the world outside its walls.

He had two main aims at St Mary's. The first was the raising of money to clean, restore and clear the building of clutter. He was responsible for placing the nave altar in the crossing between the transepts in front of the chancel. This was not a very revolutionary concept a generation later, but for this he was arraigned by the Archdeacon before the Consistory Court for not having the alterations properly 'facultied', though his action was in effect approved retrospectively. He became very critical of church lawyers as a result.

McCulloch's second and more difficult aim was the exorcising of what he called 'triumphalism', an undue pride in past glories: he believed there was no virtue in resting on other people's laurels. But by the time he left Warwick in 1959 he felt that his parishioners' pride 'was no longer so much in the beauty of the building as in the beauty of what was enacted within it'. 'We had become recognisably a body of people who belonged to each other, not because we were socially homogeneous ... but because we had come to know one another as persons who met around the Lord's Table, and took part in the Liturgy.' But a leader in the *Warwick Advertiser* at the time referred to 'the close of a notable period in the long history of St Mary's' and observed that the departing Vicar 'should be remembered less for the controversial aspects of his ministry at St Mary's than for much good solid work which escaped attention'. McCulloch commented, 'It sought to show me as having become a part of Warwick's history, and thus in the final analysis I willy-nilly had added to its triumphalism'.

However, it was when he left Warwick and became for twenty years the Rector of St Mary-le-Bow that Joseph McCulloch really hit the headlines in the eyes of the world, and was at his most effective in the service of God. Here was a situation which ideally suited him: a blitzed church building from which he could build a new church starting from scratch. 'What I saw was a carte blanche, a superb chance to pay the piper and call the tune, to fulfil a dream of building a church ... which could carry the past into the living present, and make a creative contribution towards the future pattern of the Christian ministry.' How could he do that? St Mary-le-Bow was only a titular parish; few people lived in the City, but many thousands were there during working hours. His first job was to rebuild the church, and for three years his office was a builder's hut and he commuted in from Hampstead. He decided to use the space over the vestry, between the tower and the church, to build a parsonage as part of the whole complex, so he would be 'living over the shop'. The Church existed – and still exists – for non-members, and in a non-residential weekday-working neighbourhood McCulloch wanted a church designed according to a more flexible and adaptable pattern, so as to draw in not only the occasional worshipper, but also the vast majority who ordinarily had little use for churches.

The main feature of the building was to be two equal pulpits. This had been the usual feature of the early Christian basilica where, during the Liturgy, the Epistle would be read from one and the Gospel from the other. 'But,' said McCulloch, 'I had a further use in mind. The identical pulpits admirably equipped the building for the resumption of the dialogue with the world which I saw as essential in the Church's present situation. They made it practicable for two people to enter into public discussion on equal terms.' And for the rest of his time at St Mary-le-Bow – fourteen years – he utilized his twin pulpits by organizing a series of weekly lunchtime dialogues with people in various walks of life who were interested in religion without necessarily being orthodox Christians. There was standing room only to hear McCulloch debate with the likes of Malcolm Muggeridge and Yehudi Menuhin, Enoch Powell and Bernard Levin, Joan Bakewell, Diana Rigg and Germaine Greer. His experiment was a huge success: it brought him national acclaim, and the dialogues were well attended by City office workers and provided a Christian witness which could never have been anywhere near as effective in a dead city on a Sunday. By the time McCulloch retired in 1979, he had merited the words, 'Well done, thou good and faithful servant'. And no doubt his time in Warwick had in some small way prepared him for this work and had therefore provided some indirect influence on the success of this new venture.

Joseph McCulloch, the radical churchman trapped within the establishment, the author of such significant titles as *A Parson in Revolt* and *The Faith that Must Offend,* died on 4 March 1990 in his eighty-second year. He had come a long way since the day over forty years earlier when Neville Gorton, the Bishop of Coventry, who had appointed him to stir up stuffy St Mary's, Warwick, viewed the church furniture with him and once outside opined, 'Only one thing to do. Put the whole lot in the street, and start again'.

As one obituary writer put it, 'Joe tried to do the same with the whole Church of England, but it was a bit too big to carry'.

— 28 —

Inventor of the Jet Engine

T HE greatest step forward in aviation since the beginnings of flight itself was undoubtedly the invention of the turbo-jet engine. Propulsion by a jet of hot gas has enabled aircraft to fly at far greater speeds than by piston-engine-driven propellers. The inventor of this jet engine was Frank Whittle, and today you can see exhibits illustrating its history at the Sir Frank Whittle Jet Heritage Centre at the Midland Air Museum at Coventry Airport.

Frank Whittle was born in Earlsdon, a suburb of Coventry, in June 1907, the son of Moses and Sara Alice Whittle who came from Lancashire of Wesleyan Methodist stock. They moved to Leamington in 1916 when Moses Whittle bought the grandly named one-man Leamington Valve and Piston Ring Company, and they were to remain there until about 1927 after Frank had left home, then moving a few miles to Corley Moor near the present motorway service station. After attending primary schools at Earlsdon and Milverton, the lad went to Leamington College for Boys until Christmas 1922, though it is said that he learnt more engineering by studying books at Leamington Public Library in his spare time, and by helping his father in his workshop.

Frank had always wanted to fly - he had been given a toy aeroplane as a Christmas present at the age of four! - and he was determined to get into the R.A.F. as a boy apprentice. He passed the written exam, but was turned down because he was only five feet tall. He applied to take the medical again when he had grown another three inches, but he was once again turned down on the principle of once rejected, always rejected. So determined was he, however, that he went through the whole procedure again as though he had never applied in the first place - and was accepted!

Young Whittle did so well in his three years from 1923 to 1926 as an apprentice mechanic at Cranwell that he was one of the few transferred as a Flight Cadet to the R.A.F. College there. Within two years he had learnt to fly and received a commission. In the years that followed he gained all-round training in aviation: with a fighter squadron; on a flying instructors' course; as a marine test pilot; and in charge of an engine test section. Then in 1934 he was seconded to Peterhouse, Cambridge where, two years later, despite working on the jet, he gained First Class Honours in the Mechanical Science Tripos. A year's post-graduate research followed, and then from 1937 to 1946 he was assigned to the Special Duty List which allowed him to work full time on his engine.

But to return to his earlier years: in 1928 while still at Cranwell and not yet twenty-one, he had written a thesis on 'Future Developments in Aircraft Design', and in 1930 he took out a patent for a jet engine. In the gas-turbine, the vital part of Whittle's invention, the air first enters a compressor; then the compressed air passes to a combustion chamber where it is ignited; and lastly the gases from this combustion strike the blades of the turbine, causing it to revolve. The turbine itself works the compressor, and the gases leaving the turbine still have enough energy to provide a thrust in the form of a jet - comparable to the release of air from a blown-up toy balloon.

Unfortunately the Air Ministry was not interested at the time, because there seemed no likelihood of suitable metals being devised to withstand the stresses and temperatures produced in such an engine. So, hard up for money, Whittle allowed the patent to lapse in 1935. However, the following year, with the financial backing of two colleagues, he took out new patents and formed a company called Power Jets Ltd. But at the time the Air Ministry made it clear that his work in connection with the engine was to be very much a spare-time job: it was not to conflict with his official duties. Fortunately, as it turned out, his post-graduate research year and then his appointment to the Special Duty List meant that in the end he could give his full-time attention to the project.

Power Jets Ltd. began by conducting their experiments at the British Thomson-Houston factory at Rugby, where in 1937 a static engine had its first test run. The following year the engine-testing site was moved to Lutterworth in Leicestershire, where the local police became suspicious, thinking Whittle might be an I.R.A. terrorist using the premises to make bombs! As it was, financial constraints and disputes between the firms involved continued to dog the project over the years. And when you consider that in 1940 the Ministry of Aircraft Production had to take the short-term view and concentrate on those aircraft already in production to the exclusion of prototype projects, it was indeed remarkable that Whittle's project was allowed to continue. But he pressed on, believing that Britain would be attacked sooner or later by very high-altitude bombers and that the only effective defence against them would be jet fighters.

After taxiing trials, Britain beat the Germans to it: our first jet aircraft, the Gloster/Whittle E28, the precursor of the Gloster Meteor (now in the Science Museum), made its first unobtrusive but successful test flight at Cranwell on 15 May 1941 - the first time that an aeroplane

Gloster–Whittle E28: the first jet-propelled aircraft.

had flown without a propeller! Further trials took place, some of them on Warwickshire's Edgehill where King and Parliament had fought it out three centuries before. Power Jets continued to expand: there were some 600 staff in 1943, by which time the design headquarters had moved to Brownsover Hall, near Rugby, and the factory to Whetstone, near Leicester.

Whittle was, however, never to be given complete control of his brainchild. The Air Ministry decided that Power Jets was not to manufacture the final product, but merely to research experimental engines. The actual building of the engines was given to British Thomson-Houston and Rover, and later to Rolls-Royce, with General Electric constructing them in the U.S.A. And then in 1944 Power Jets, but no other gas-turbine firm, was nationalized. In fact, because of engine problems and unnecessary political factors, the first Meteor jet was not delivered to the R.A.F. until May 1944. It was used initially for shooting down the V1 flying bombs. The Vampire jet followed. And now virtually all military and passenger aircraft are 'jet' rather than 'prop'.

Whittle first flew a jet himself in October 1945. But all the hard work and, perhaps more so, the years of negotiating with sceptical public bodies, had taken their toll on his health. Disillusioned with the new management, he resigned from Power Jets in 1946, and in 1948 he was invalided out of the R.A.F. with the rank of Air Commodore and made a Knight Commander of the British Empire. The same year he received an award of £100,000 free of tax on the recommendation of the Royal Commission on Awards to Inventors.

Subsequent honours included the Award of Merit of the City of Coventry, the Honorary Freedom of the Borough of Royal Leamington Spa and nine honorary doctorates. Finally, having emigrated to the U.S.A. in 1976, he was made a member of our select twenty-four-man Order of Merit in 1986, and in 1991 his jet fighter appeared in a set of postage stamps dedicated to pioneers of science; belated tributes to the Warwickshire lad who had revolutionized air travel.

— 29 —

Anti-Nuclear Campaigner

OVER the years the name of Pat Arrowsmith, peace campaigner and Socialist, has hit the national headlines. She was born in Leamington on 2 March 1930, when her father, Revd G. E. Arrowsmith, was Vicar of St Paul's. Since her days at Cheltenham Ladies' College ('I went to boarding school, the perfect training for prison') and Newnham College, Cambridge, she has worked in a variety of jobs from child care officer and psychiatric nursing assistant to waitress and typist, cinema usherette and farmhand. Since 1971 she has worked for Amnesty International, being adopted by them twice as a prisoner of conscience. Way back she was a member of the Direct Action Committee against Nuclear War which organized the first Aldermaston march in 1958. Miss Arrowsmith has been a prominent member of the Campaign for Nuclear Disarmament (she is currently a Vice-President), and as such she has been dumped into an icy pool on a rocket base, hosed down from the side of a Polaris submarine and forcibly fed in prison. Since 1958 she has been jailed twelve times, always refusing to be bound over: in May 1974 she got eighteen months for distributing leaflets to soldiers urging the withdrawal of troops from Northern Ireland. She has stood three times as an Independent candidate at general elections, the last time in 1979 as an Independent Socialist against Prime Minister James Callaghan in Cardiff South-East. However, she joined the Labour Party in 1980 when it adopted a policy of unilateral nuclear disarmament, but resigned from it in 1989 when the party changed to a multilateral stance.

Miss Arrowsmith has always maintained that she is opposed to war from any source. She 'invaded' the Soviet Embassy in London in 1968 when Russian tanks moved into Czechoslovakia, and she later staged a week's fast outside the same embassy. She also went to East Germany during the Cold War and painted slogans there revealing the whereabouts of secret missile bases.

When she wanted to go on a month's holiday to the United States, the American Embassy told her that to get a visa she must supply a full list of court convictions, with certificates from the clerks of the courts. After she had written down the Central Criminal Court, Bow Street, Marylebone, Willesden, Ealing, Braintree, Swaffham, Norwich, Bootle, Edinburgh and Dunoon, her memory failed her. But would that not be sufficient for the embassy? No, it would not. And so she had to engage in a tortuous correspondence. But she got her visa in the end!

It was characteristic of Pat Arrowsmith that when refusing to pay a £71 fine she paid the same amount to a Live Aid Appeal instead. It was equally characteristic that she established a Peace Camp in the Gulf during the recent war. She wrote to *The Guardian* (15 October 1990) at the head of a list of signatories for the Gulf Peace Team:

> We are concerned at the prospect of war in the Gulf. By going to the area and setting up a peace camp or some form of non-violent presence we hope to make a small contribution to the efforts of ordinary people to prevent war. We should like to hear from anyone willing to support this project.

A month later she left Heathrow for Jordan and from there went to Baghdad. Pat Arrowsmith and her colleagues – eventually to number some seventy people from fifteen countries – proceeded to set up their Peace Camp on the Saudi-Kuwait border in an effort to disrupt the movement of the military on both sides. It was a non-violent protest in the Gandhi tradition, terminated only when Saddam Hussein forced them to leave at the height of the conflict.

Miss Arrowsmith has continued to protest against war in all its forms right up to the present. In May 1992 she was among the leaders of the group Active Resistance to the Roots of War, who demonstrated against the controversial erection of a statue to Sir Arthur 'Bomber' Harris, architect of the policy of area bombing in the Second World War.

Pat Arrowsmith's grandparents were missionaries who were stoned to death in China. Their grand-daughter is also willing to take risks. She is a very different character from Frances Ridley Havergal, that other lady connected with St Paul's in Leamington, but similarly she has shown the courage of her convictions – and is prepared to suffer for it.

So Pat Arrowsmith's story is still being told.

Bibliography

Aitken, Leslie *Massacre on the Road to Dunkirk* (Patrick Stephens, 2nd ed., 1988).

Arch, Joseph *Autobiography* (MacGibbon and Kee, 1966). (Originally published as *Joseph Arch: the Story of his Life; told by himself*, Hutchinson, 1898, and later reissued as *From Ploughtail to Parliament*, Cresset Library, 1986.)

Bingham, Caroline *The Life and Times of Edward II* (Weidenfield & Nicolson, 1973).

Bird, Michael *Samuel Shepheard of Cairo* (Michael Joseph, 1957).

Bloom, James Harvey *The Errors of the Avon Star: Another Literary Manual for the Stratford-on-Avon Season of 1903* (John Morgan, Stratford, 1903).
   — *The Story of Warwickshire* (Pitman).

Bloom, Ursula *The Changed Village* (Chapman & Hall, 1945).
   — *The Elegant Edwardian* (Hutchinson, 1957).
   — *Life is no Fairy Tale* (1976).
   — *Parson Extraordinary* (Hale, 1963).
   — *Rosemary for Stratford* (Hale, 1966).

Blunden Margaret *The Countess of Warwick* (Cassell, 1967).
   — *The Educational and Political Work of the Countess of Warwick* (unpublished thesis, 1965).

Burgess, Alan *Seven Men at Daybreak* (Evans Bros., 1960).

Catlin, George *For God's Sake, Go!* (Colin Smythe, 1972).

Catlin, John *Family Quartet: Vera Brittain and Her Family* (Hamish Hamilton, 1987).

Colvin, Sidney *Landor* (Macmillan, 1881, English Men of Letters Series).

Corelli, Marie *The Avon Star: a Literary Manual for the Stratford-on-Avon Season of 1903* (A. J. Stanley, Stratford, 1903).

Derry, Warren *Dr Parr: a Portrait of the Whig Dr Johnson* (Oxford University Press, 1966).

Dictionary of National Biography.

Dodge, Walter Phelps *Piers Gaveston: a Chapter of Early Constitutional History* (T. Fisher Unwin, 1899).

Dugdale, Thomas *The Antiquities of Warwickshire* (2nd ed., 1730).

Elwin, Malcolm *Landor: a Replevin* (Macdonald, 1958).

Focus - various articles.

Gibbons, W. G. *Royal Leamington Spa, Part III: Signs of the Past* (Jones-Sands, 1986).
— *Royal Leamington Spa: The Seeds of Lawn Tennis* (Jones-Sands, 1986).

Golley, John *Whittle: the True Story* (Airlife Publishing Ltd., 1987).

Green, David *Gardener to Queen Anne* (Oxford University Press, 1956).

Grierson, Janet *Frances Ridley Havergal: Worcestershire Hymnwriter* (Havergal Society, 1979).

Hamilton, J. S. *Piers Gaveston, Earl of Cornwall, 1307-1312: Politics and Patronage in the Reign of Edward II* (Harvester Wheatsheaf, 1988).

Holt, Tonie and Valmai *In Search of the Better 'Ole: the Life, Works and Collectables of Bruce Bairnsfather* (Milestone, 1985).

Horn, Pamela *Joseph Arch (1826-1919): the Farm Workers' Leader* (Roundwood Press, 1971).

Jones, Mary Whitmore *The Gunpowder Plot and Life of Robert Catesby: also an Account of Chastleton House* (Thomas Burleigh, 1909).

Lang, Theo *My Darling Daisy* (Michael Joseph, 1966).

Lines, Charles *The Book of Warwick* (Barracuda Books, 1985).

Lloyd, T. H. 'Dr Wade and the Working Class' in *Midland History*, Vol. ii, No. 2 (Autumn 1973), pp 61-83.

McCulloch, Joseph *My Affair with the Church* (Hodder & Stoughton, 1976).

Macdonald, Callum *The Killing of S.S. Obergruppenfuhrer Reinhard Heydrich, 27 May 1942* (Macmillan, 1989).

Masters, Brian *Now Barabbas was a Rotter: the Extraordinary Life of Marie Corelli* (Hamish Hamilton, 1978).

Nelson, Nina *Shepheard's Hotel* (Barrie and Rockliffe, 1960).

New Grove Dictionary of Music and Musicians.

Newbold, E. B. *Portrait of Coventry* (Hale, 1972).
— *Warwickshire History Makers* (E.P. Publishing, 1975).

Oxford Companion to the Theatre.

Parkinson, C. Northcote *Gunpowder, Treason and Plot* (Weidenfield & Nicolson, 1976).

Roe, Lucy M. *William Croft, 1678-1727: Tercentenary Celebrations 1978.*
— 'William Croft & His Warwickshire Background' in *Warwickshire History*, Vol. iv, No. 4 (Winter 1979/80), pp132-145.

Sayer, Ian, and Botting, Douglas *Hitler's Last General: the Case against Wilhelm Mohnke* (Bantam Press, 1989).

Smith, Betty *Tales of Old Stratford* (Countryside Books, 1988).
— *Tales of Old Warwickshire* (Countryside Books, 1989).

Vickers, Kenneth H. *England in the Later Middle Ages* (Methuen, 1913).

Vyver, Bertha *Memoirs of Marie Corelli* (Alston Rivers, 1930).

Wade, Arthur Savage *A Voice from the Church: or a Sermon... on Church Reform...* (James Ridgway, London, 1832).

Warwick and Warwickshire Advertiser.

Warwickshire and Worcestershire Life - various articles.
Whittle, Frank *Jet: the Story of a Pioneer* (Muller, 1953).
Who's Who.

Acknowledgements

The quotation from 'Sea Fever' by John Masefield is reproduced by permission of the Society of Authors.

Illustrations are reproduced by permission of the following:
  Camera Press;
  Clive Carey;
  Tonie and Valmai Holt;
  The Science Museum;
  Warwickshire and Worcestershire Life;
  Warwickshire County Library;
  Warwickshire County Record Office;
  Wimbledon Lawn Tennis Museum;
  Chris Wright.

Other photographs are by Doreen Bolitho.

The author wishes to express his appreciation to Pat Dunlop for her advice on the preparation of this book for publication.